Mercy in Weakness

Mercy in Weakness

Meditations on the Word

———

ANDRÉ LOUF

Translator: John Vriend

DARTON · LONGMAN + TODD

First published in 1998 by
Darton, Longman and Todd Ltd
1 Spencer Court
140–142 Wandsworth High Street
London SW18 4JJ

ISBN 0–232–52104–2

A catalogue record for this book is available
from the British Library.

Designed by Sandie Boccacci
Phototypeset in 11/13.5pt Ehrhardt by Intype London Ltd
Printed and bound in Great Britain by
Page Bros, Norwich

Contents

CONTENTS

Preface

These 'meditations' were first written to be communicated orally. Most of them originate from homilies preached in recent years on the gospel readings for ordinary Sundays of the year. All of them therefore are the fruit of an appreciative and contemplative rumination on the Word of God.

What else can the preacher of the Word proffer, other than that which has touched and wounded his heart, during his own private and personal *lectio divina*? This sweet and gentle wound is, in his eyes, the sign of the Spirit prompting him to a word of edification, calling him to gather together and to effectively build up the liturgical assembly, the real Church of today, present before him.

When he spoke, the author of these lines was first addressing his brothers – the monks of his own community – even though, particularly on Sundays and feast days, they are joined by a large crowd of other worshippers who are not involved in the monastic life. In spite of that, and with no hesitations, he gave priority to addressing the monks. Their concerns, their difficulties and temptations, as well as their hopes, are set before the light and strength issuing from the Word of God. So these texts echo first of all an interior journey that is specifically contemplative, and deal only in passing with the various questions which stir our times and challenge a Church that is uncompromisingly present at the heart of the world.

Yet the source of the light that these words seek to reflect is always the words of Jesus himself. So this light can never be totally foreign to the experience of all those who are involved in the varied occupations of life in the midst of the world. Poring patiently and lovingly over the insights of the gospel in this way, brings us inescapably to the core of all Christian experience, whether it is lived in close contact with the world or at a greater distance from it, in monastic solitude. In fact, monks and nuns are just as much at the heart of the world; differently, to be sure, but no less effectively. Letting ourselves be possessed by the Word, so that we may be transformed by it into praise and intercession, or may bear witness to it before others, requires, in both cases, the same familiarity with it.

In both cases, too, we soon become aware of what is the quintessence of any authentically Christian faith, of the only light that can guide us to the very end of the path of faith: God's great love, wherever it may lead us, prefers us first to be poor and naked, before tenderly showering his gifts and his joy upon us. Rather than sating us immediately beyond anything we dare imagine, God's joy first divests us radically. It can sometimes take us years to understand this, whether we are hidden in a cloister or out on the highways proclaiming the Word of God: until the day we capitulate and hand ourselves over to an almighty One who takes delight in our weakness.

Hence the title given to this collection of texts. To illustrate it with a testimony from the Fathers, we have chosen a passage of Bernard of Clairvaux, in which one day he expressed one of his most luminous insights into the gospels. He gave it form in that brilliant writing of his, so deeply moving, so full of the echoes of countless Scripture texts.

How many lives of saints, apostles or mystics, throughout the ages, have poignantly testified to this luminous insight:

> What a desirable weakness that is compensated by the strength of Christ! Who will give me not only to be weak, but more, to be totally overthrown and debased in my own eyes, so as to be grounded in the might of the Lord Almighty? For power is made perfect in weakness. That is why Scripture says: It is when I am weak that I am the strongest and the mightiest.
>
> (St Bernard, *Sermons on the Song of Songs*, 25, 7)

André Louf

1

The Place Where Miracles Happen

The Word of God is pervaded by an irresistible force. It never misses its goal, nor does it return to God without having accomplished its mission. This is something the parable of the sower (Matt. 13:1–23) teaches us.

Indeed, the Word is full of God's own life: potent life which in a mysterious way, like that of a seed, bears within itself the full-grown tree and the ripe fruit. Normally it is enough for us to let nature take its course and unfold its potencies. Each little seed, however small, will one day germinate. First it will become a blade, then produce a stem, next leaves, and finally flowers and fruit – undisturbed, each in its own time. For this process to unfold no outside force is needed, Jesus once commented (Mark 4:26–9). All a person needs to do is scatter the seed on the field; then he can go home to rest or sleep. The seed will sprout of its own accord and produce fruit. That's how it goes with the omnipotent life of the Father which is present in every word about him that is tirelessly sown in our hearts by the Bible and the liturgy. That is the first conclusion we can draw.

However, this initial conclusion seems to be called into question. It needs, at the very least, to be supplemented by a second, one which is the precise point of the parable of the sower. After all, the vigorous life of God can by mistake be frustrated by inattention, inadequate preparation, or by the distractedness of those who should be ready to receive it. At work here is an awesome force, perhaps even a counterforce present in humans, to which God takes the risk of exposing himself. The miracles he wants to accomplish by his Word can be negated and perhaps come to nothing on account of a person's inattention. The same human being who was above all destined, called and chosen by God to become his instrument is perhaps no more than an obstacle standing in God's way, preventing the completion of the miracle. For God has once-and-for-all decided to honour human freedom and not to work a single miracle against a person's will. If necessary, he is prepared to sow his Word on hardened soil, soil that is incapable of bringing forth fruit.

Certainly it is clear that, for it to germinate and grow, every little seed needs soft soil in which to die and then spring into new life for the coming harvest. The trampled soil of the road, ground that is too rocky, and fallow land overgrown by thistles and weeds, are not suited for this purpose. This is how it is with the Word of Life which the divine Sower is eager to entrust to us. In a heart that is jammed up and hardened by cares and worries, sated with riches, and disturbed by a person's own ambition and rivalry, the Word is doomed to vegetate poorly and never really to unfold; it will be perpetually threatened by the death of strangulation. The Sower is not to blame: every day he goes out to sow the seed with a full hand and a generous swing; the soil which is not prepared and therefore incapable of giving the life of God a chance to grow is responsible.

Again, in any case we are dealing with an awesome power. On the one hand, the power hidden in the Word of God is given free course so that it becomes, among brothers, a source of life and the place where miracles happen. On the other hand, there is also another power which blocks the coming of God's miracles, usually not from weakness or intentionally, but simply from inattention. It is amply sufficient, however, for a person to turn with an unencumbered heart and full of attentiveness to God, to let him multiply the fruit, a hundredfold, sixtyfold, or thirtyfold.

2

God Surprises Us

'Good news, a great joy for all the people: today a Saviour has been born for you . . . the Messiah, the Lord' (Luke 2:10, 11). For centuries people had been looking for this event: now God fulfilled his promise. But the event was still a complete surprise. The promise which became a reality surpassed everything people had ever dared to hope.

Yet, the people of God knew it and the whole Bible witnesses to it: a number of times, in the course of the history of salvation God had made the barren womb bear fruit at last. Numerous women, from Rebekah to Elizabeth, Mary's aged relative, had given thanks to God for it. This happened even to the degree that every unexpected birth, every birth outside of the usual possibilities of a woman, had begun to amount to something like an announcement and a symbol of the salvation which God would one day grant his people. 'Raise a glad cry, you barren one who did not bear . . . For more numerous are the children of the deserted wife than the children of her who has a husband,' Isaiah had foretold (54:1). And elsewhere he had said: 'the virgin shall bear a son and shall name him Immanuel, "With us is God" ' (7:14).

Up to this point the extraordinary was ordinary, one could say, because throughout their entire history the Jews had acclaimed all these marvellous births as miracles of God's inexhaustible love. But by the birth on this Christmas night the boundaries of the inconceivable and completely improbable were crossed. This helpless child *is* the Lord; he is God himself. This very last time God surpassed himself in omnipotence, love and ingenuity – something of which the angel Gabriel had already assured Mary when he said: 'To God nothing is impossible' (Luke 2:37).

Indeed, in this helpless little child, who cries in his cradle or, bunched up on his young mother's lap, finds comfort at her breast, God's look becomes visible, marvellously surprising, beyond all expectation, totally unforeseen. He is, in the first place, *a miracle of truth*, for this child is not an angel of God, or a new prophet, one specially sent by God, but the Son of the God who so loved the world that he now gave his own Son. He is *a miracle of nearness*, too, because the Son of God is now squarely among us, in a body like ours, a body we can see, meet, touch, caress, a body which will one day be delivered up to our blows and scorn by a traitor's kiss. Finally, he is *a divine surprise of God's love* which always culminates in the fulfilment of everything that surpasses our expectations.

This is one of the traits of God who is occupied with his people. It is a trait which stands out even more vividly on this Christmas night and which is mysteriously present in our life every day, assuring us that it is he who is with us: the God who always astonishes and surprises us anew. His deeds are marvellous; they surpass everything we ever dared hope. However long the preceding nights may have been – and both God and humanity had to wait centuries before this night of Christmas could finally be bathed in light – and however dark they were, the history of salvation and our human history inescapably ended in fruitfulness.

That is the joyful message of the night of Christmas: if the little child who was born in Bethlehem is truly the Son of God, then from that moment on everything becomes possible. Then the outlook of the world will change, every hurt will have meaning because it will be healed, every cloud of darkness will be swept away by the light, and every sorrow turn into joy. For in this little child of Christmas God's grace is revealed for the salvation of all. From this point on every human weakness will be clothed with the power of God's Son, cherished and caressed by his love.

3

Hidden Grace

'The grace of God has appeared on earth, bringing salvation to all' (Titus 2:11). These words of St Paul are in full accord with the words the angels addressed to the shepherds on this night: 'I proclaim to you good news of great joy that is meant for all the people. For today in the city of David a Saviour has been born for you, who is the Messiah, the Lord' (Luke 2:10–12).

The grace of God has appeared on earth! The grace of God: that is his goodness and love. But what does it mean that it appeared on earth? To know that one is loved is one thing; to feel loved is something else. There is a vast difference between talk about love and the concrete experience of that love. Ever since the time of the patriarchs the people of God knew they were borne up by grace. From now on the grace of God has appeared in Jesus; it has become visible; we can feel it. It has come among us, even within the reach of our senses. It has taken on human form so that henceforth every human being can observe it.

Grace has indeed appeared on earth. Yet it is not entirely simple to observe it immediately; we could almost say that it is not visible to the naked eye. 'And this will be a sign for you,' the angel says to the shepherds, 'an infant in a manger.' In like manner the unusually brilliant star which leads the wise men to the child is a sign. Without a sign from God, grace might still pass by unnoticed, even though it is revealed and made visible, as happens at Christmas. For it is both visible and hidden. It does not glitter, nor blind anyone's eyes. It seems even to wrap itself in unthought-of forms and to hide itself where it is not expected.

Sometimes, for example, it appears at night and not in broad daylight. It does not become visible in full majesty but in the lowly and total dependence of a new-born child, 'wrapped in swaddling clothes and lying in a manger'. 'Who has believed what we have heard?' cried the prophet Isaiah. This Christmas night, however, is only the first step on the road to the revelation of grace. One day we will be confronted with it, no longer in the charm of a small child, but in the disfigured face of the suffering servant, as the same Isaiah says: 'Neither his external bearing nor beauty were worth looking at; nor was his appearance such that it attracted people. He was spurned and avoided by men, a man of sorrows' (Isa. 53:2, 3). One day we too will have to reconcile ourselves to that strange grace and love which become perfectly clear only in death, for there is no greater love and no greater grace than for him to give his life for others. This grace has been revealed to us, yet is always still hidden from us. We must try ever more deeply to enter into it and to experience it more intensely at every Christmas.

This is our privilege on the holy night of Christmas, as we again listen to the story of Jesus' birth and celebrate this event in the mystery of the Eucharist. This grace has been granted in abundance, yet there are so many people who celebrate Christmas without understanding what it is all about: thus the grace that has been revealed always remains hidden as well.

Even to us this grace is still hidden in part, perhaps even for the most part. For it is only very gradually revealed to us, even though every Christmas celebration offers us a chance to feel more intensely the inexpressible marvel of it all, both around and in us, but often in places where we would not expect it at all: around us, among the smallest and poorest, and also within ourselves, in the deepest part of ourselves where the birth of Jesus, the Word of God, ceaselessly repeats itself. Usually this happens without our being conscious of it, without our feeling it, down in the humblest and deepest layers of what we carry within ourselves: the poor, tiny child which determines our most basic identity and which we can only recover and accept by grace, the same child we will be for all eternity, dwelling together with Jesus in the heart of his Father.

4

Peaceful Omnipotence

After living for thirty years in the seclusion of life at home with Joseph and Mary, Jesus left his family in Nazareth. For the first time he came into contact with the public, and that first public appearance did not go unnoticed. On the contrary, it was an immediate hit, a bull's-eye: people were enthusiastic, having never before heard anyone speak as Jesus did. Jesus' public instruction was not at all like that of the scribes, who only repeated themselves. They indeed stuck to the Law and the Prophets. But Jesus spoke 'as one who had authority', according to Mark (1:21–8).

'With authority' means two things: first, that Jesus spoke in his own name, and secondly, that his words established a bond between himself and his listeners. They not only heard a message but were touched in the depths of their hearts. As well as being convincing, Jesus also conquered their hearts: his words were irresistible.

All the testimonies about Jesus are completely in agreement on this point: he could not remain hidden even if he wanted to. A mysterious power proceeded from him through his words and deeds. When the most astute among the Jews began to suspect who he was – 'You are the Messiah, the Holy One of God' – Jesus intervened and commanded them to keep the secret to themselves.

And there was more: not only was there an unheard-of power in his words, his presence alone already unsettled people. It was enough for Jesus to appear at any given place to flush out the 'adversary', also called the prince of this world. It was this adversary whom Jesus, by his advent into the world, had come to combat and drive out. Jesus had only to appear at any given place for everything that resembled that mysterious adversary to be startled and come out of hiding as though it wanted to measure itself against Jesus' strength. Jesus cast out demons, kept preaching the gospel, healed the sick, brought the dead back to life and went about doing good. His public actions and appearances were never innocuous or devoid of danger. And the Jews, who felt completely defeated and embarrassed, asked themselves: 'What is this? A new teaching – with authority! He commands even the unclean spirits and they obey him.'

And all this is happening already at the beginning of Jesus' healing and redeeming activity. We are still very far from Golgotha, still far removed from the morning of his resurrection, but simply by his presence Jesus is already extremely effective. He quietly goes his way as an irresistible Redeemer.

At the moment of his departure from the world Jesus entrusted this same persuasiveness to his disciples and to his Church. This means he imparted this gift to each one of us right up to this day. Moreover, he promised that those who would believe in him would do even greater things than he had done. It would be enough for them to put their faith and trust in him. Also, it would be useless for them to try to resist the upwelling powers and to rely on their own light. If the situation was such that words had to be spoken and a witness had to be given, the Spirit of Jesus himself would give the disciples the right words to say.

Wherever a disciple of Jesus passes by, evil too will be around and come out of hiding. Protests, contradiction, opposition, rejection, disasters, persecutions – none of this will be lacking, and all for the sake of Jesus' Name and in accordance with his promise. But neither will Jesus' power ever be lacking: 'In my name you will drive out demons, lay hands on the sick, and they will be healed (Mark 16:17); 'And the gates of hell will never overpower you' (Matt. 16:18).

For disciples of Jesus it is enough, every day anew, to place their feet in the footprints of Jesus, to take up his cross and to follow him wherever he goes. 'Be confident,' Jesus also tells us, 'I have conquered the world.' And St John adds to this: 'And the weapon with which we conquer the world is no other than our faith' (1 John 5:4).

5

Only Love Engenders Love

From the beginning of his public ministry Jesus surrounded himself with disciples whom he picked as he saw fit. Their names are known to us and they became famous as well. We know the background and even the occupation of several of them.

By what criteria did Jesus select them? At first glance, the diversity of their background makes it rather hard to give a simple answer to this question. The account in Matthew's gospel (4:12–22) furnishes only a few elements of an answer. We see Jesus at work at the moment he summoned the best known of his disciples: Peter and Andrew, John and James. This event occurred on the lakeshore and the men who were called were fishermen busy mending their nets in the company of their father. It is a short but very lively passage; in a moment the whole event is over. Jesus' crisp summons was followed in each case by an entirely spontaneous answer on the part of the future disciple. Completely unexpectedly he descended in their lives and they responded to the summons without offering an iota of resistance, without prior deliberation, without raising questions or posing conditions, as if everything just happened spontaneously or had been agreed upon long before. As we look at this scene from a distance, it seems to us like something unexpected, improvised, almost unpredictable. In any case, it is not easy to understand.

A related passage in Mark's gospel (3:13–19) tells us a

little more about the possible motives for this brusque act of interference on the part of Jesus. He writes that 'Jesus called to him those whom he himself wanted'. The selection, accordingly, does not come from the side of those called; it proceeds in the first place from Jesus himself. It is he who wants them or does not want them, an expression which clearly indicates that in this selection Jesus enjoys supreme freedom. No one can oblige him or put any pressure on him. No self-interest plays a role in the choices he makes. A person was simply selected because Jesus preferred him, without any further motives. Jesus chooses the rich and the poor, Jewish nationalists and collaborators, ordinary people and fishermen. At the moment of selection what matters is not what these people are. He simply prefers them because he loves them, each one individually. Nothing other than Jesus' love and preference explains this selection. A similar supreme freedom in the love of Jesus explains the persuasive power of his conduct. It also tells us something about the speed with which the future apostles must respond to his summons. Jesus could have persuaded them in an entirely different manner – by a fiery speech, for example, or by irrefutable arguments, by extraordinary promises or by the irresistible radiance of his personality. But had he resorted to such means he would not really have respected them. In that case he would have been putting pressure on them and so desecrated the sanctuary of their freedom. Then, sooner or later, this initial fervent enthusiasm of his disciples would have turned against him. At the first difficulties they would probably have felt that Jesus had pulled a fast one on them and betrayed their deepest desire; they would have felt more like slaves than true companions, something they would never have forgiven him for.

Only a gratuitous and completely disinterested love could

so profoundly and swiftly persuade them. Only a completely free love could arouse a love which was equally free and spontaneous. Love can only unfold completely in a heart which is fully expectant and open, in the intimate and hidden place in every human being where freedom still slumbers unconsciously. Only love can engender love, a love which will never regret anything, whatever happens; a love, strong as death, which will never be quenched, either by a flood of temptations or by the storm of death. It is because Jesus wanted us that he chose us. And because he wanted us, we on our part can also choose him, everyday anew, without withdrawing into the shell of self, without bitterness or regret. What counts is that we entrust ourselves to his love, a love which is always the first to choose.

6

God, too, Wants To Be Weak

To believe in Jesus always means to lay oneself open and take risks. Despite appearing to be the reverse, it is as if one exposes oneself to the incomprehension of the public, sometimes to the point of being ridiculous. Still more, however, it means surrendering oneself to Jesus and his omnipotence. And for Jesus, too, to be believed is to expose himself to humans. In the sphere of faith both Jesus and the believer find themselves at the nethermost point of their weakness. There they encounter each other and there the miracle can happen.

The gospel shows us two such believers: a leader of the synagogue, named Jairus, whose little daughter was at the point of death, and a woman who had long suffered from haemorrhages and received no benefit from human physicians (Mark 5:21–43). Both had to brave the unbelief and derisive laughter of the crowd to give themselves up to Jesus.

First there is Jairus. He faces his friends who have seen with their own eyes that his daughter is dead and want to keep him from further pressing his case before Jesus. They even go so far as to laugh at him when Jesus says that his daughter is only sleeping.

Then there is the woman. How much courage must it have taken for her to push her way through that crowd of people in the quiet hope of being able secretly to touch Jesus' cloak. And suddenly she is confronted by the unbelief of the apostles who are astonished when among all those people Jesus is looking for someone who touched him: 'You see the crowd pressing in on you from all directions and you ask: "Who touched me?" ' In that crush of people there were many who had touched Jesus, but someone had awakened a healing power in his body. One individual in that crowd had power over Jesus, because she had touched him by faith.

To Jairus, as well as to the woman who had suffered from haemorrhages, Jesus spoke only about believing in him. Nothing is improbable or impossible for one who believes. To Jairus, who was at the point of collapsing when he learned of the irrevocable death of his daughter, Jesus simply said: 'Be not afraid, only keep believing.' And to the sick woman who was embarrassed because she had been caught doing something which seemed rather childish, Jesus said: 'Daughter, your faith has made you whole.' In the first case, it was not Jesus' omnipotence at issue but Jairus' faith. Nor was the healing power of Jesus in question in the case of the sick woman, but only her faith.

Not that Jesus was not omnipotent. He clearly was, but he never used his omnipotence to his own advantage. Nor does he use it for his own pleasure as a professional healer might. Jesus' omnipotence is simply at the disposal of those who touch him, who touch his heart by believing in him: 'Don't be afraid, but keep believing. Your faith has made you whole.' While Jesus certainly is almighty, he is more than that: he yields to the faith of a man or a woman; he is extremely vulnerable to anyone who puts his or her trust in him. One could say he deliberately chooses not to employ his omnipotence in order to make room for the power of our faith.

That precisely is the paradoxical nature of God's love. He

decides that the place of his omnipotence is first of all the place of his weakness. He accepts the fact that it is impossible for him to work a miracle where our faith defaults. Our faith, the faith that gives him joy, is his strength as well. 'Be not afraid, only keep believing.' All things are possible to one who believes. Faith, after all, amounts to loving surrender, the firm confidence of one who knows himself or herself beloved. But it is above all, as in the case of Jesus, power in extreme weakness. It is not the person who knows and is able to do things, who judges and condemns who practises faith. By believing, a human being yields and surrenders, lowers his arms and drops his weapons; with his whole body and all his possessions he delivers himself up to love. As St Paul puts it, the joy of love is – the time still given us is – to live by faith in the Son of God who first loved us and gave himself for us (see Gal. 2:20).

7

Precious Time

Three times during his discourse to the disciples Jesus tells them to stay awake. 'Stay awake, for you do not know when the moment will come . . . And what I say to you, I say to all: stay awake!' (Mark 13:33–7)

The history of humankind is marked by this waiting and watching, just like time, which is meant to encompass the encounter between God and humanity. God himself had no need for time, but he created it the moment he made a human being to facilitate meeting him or her at a certain time. The encounter with a creature, after all, must necessarily occur at a well-defined point in time and each creature now prepares himself or herself for this moment by waiting for it. We live for and toward this moment, full of hope, fixing our minds on what is to come.

In the course of history time has twice been given to us by God with a view to our waiting for him. The first time this occurred in connection with Jesus' first coming. For centuries the Jews had waited and looked for a Messiah who would come to redeem Israel. All events in history were viewed and interpreted in the light of this expectation. By successive series of kings and prophets the image of the Messiah gradually became clearer. This continued until time was fulfilled and humanity was able to receive and recognise God's own Son. For by Jesus God himself came to visit his people. His coming altered the course of history.

When he left the world to return to his Father, Jesus left

behind an indelible sign on earth. Not only did he do this by his deeds and actions, neither did he do this only by the Word he entrusted to his Church, he did this especially by leaving to us the legacy of his own life, the Holy Spirit, the Spirit of the Son and the Father who dwells among us and whose presence, though hidden, will considerably accelerate the time remaining. From now on the time is short, for love compels us. Time has been given to us so that we can again await the coming of God, the return of our Lord Jesus to this earth.

In this hour, which is the hour of the Church, time is visibly ripening. Jesus is ever coming closer. The years succeed each other ever more swiftly and they hasten to plunge us, so to speak, into the arms of Jesus. This hour naturally remains concealed from us for until the time has been fulfilled it is known only to the Father as a secret of love and compassion which he is preparing for each one of us. The only thing we know is that it will happen unexpectedly, like a thief's coming in the night, says Jesus, and woe to the careless ones who have fallen asleep. Or as Jesus puts it elsewhere, this coming is unexpected like that of the bridegroom who arrives at night (Matt. 25:1–13). For we only wait well and watch well when we are impelled to do so by love.

How precious, then, is this time in which we may live with what is to us the most treasured thing in the world: our desire to see the Lord. For time is meant to awaken, intensify and deepen our longing. The closer we come to Jesus, the more frequently it seems to us that we are farther removed from him than ever. The more nakedly immediate the encounter with him is, the more relentlessly the years seem to drag on. Time makes us humble before God. First he purifies our all-too-impetuous enthusiasm, then he gradually brings us back to what is fundamental: the passionate but peaceful waiting for him whom we love and who awaits us even more than we can ever await him.

It is important that we never try to manage time sneakily; that would mean we were trying to outwit God. Nor must we ever try to break the flow of time, for in so doing we might run the risk of cutting ourselves off from God. Quietly and humbly we must stand up to time, refuse to be led astray by it, and not let ourselves be distracted by mundane or vulgar amusements. God is greater than time, greater also than our waiting, just as he is greater than our heart. He, however, dwells in our time until, with the coming of Jesus, this time will pass into eternity. And Jesus will come, when he wills, as he wills and where he wills. 'And what I say to you, I say to all: stay awake!'

8

The Second Baptism

The people who listened to John the Baptist were invited to live between two baptisms (Matt. 3:1–12). First there was the baptism in water which the prophet in the desert offered for the forgiveness of their sins. But this first baptism was not to be the last. After John Jesus will come; he will be greater and stronger than John and he will administer a new baptism which will be radically decisive: a baptism with the Holy Spirit and fire. A fire that burns to turn into ashes all that does not produce good fruit – a fire that will not lead to death but to life. For it is the Holy Spirit himself who purifies, who consumes all disaffection and apostasy, who will make people 'red-hot' and melt them in order to create more durable forms.

Jesus himself lived between two baptisms. For him too there was initially a baptism in water administered by the same John the Baptist. It was, however, infinitely more effective than the baptism that other Jews received at the hands of John. The heavens opened above Jesus and the Father broke his silence to baptise him and to take him up into his divine love – 'In you I have my delight' – and to anoint him with his Spirit, the Spirit who would dwell in him from that time on.

For Jesus, too, this first baptism would not be his last. It merely opened the road to Easter, the road he had to travel because it ended in a second and radically decisive baptism: that of his blood in the waters of death. That was a baptism

of which he was one day to say that he so passionately
desired it that his soul would remain anguished until the
hour of its accomplishment. The baptism of Jesus, which
began by his immersion in the waters of the Jordan river,
ends in his doleful yet glorious Easter, the mystery of the
redemption and transformation of humanity, to become
the source and mystery-filled reality of our baptism today.

For we, on our part, were baptised with the sacrament of
baptism as well. That was also a baptism in water but with
a scope and effectiveness that go far beyond the baptism
which John the Baptist administered in his day. It bears
within itself, in a mysterious fashion, the entire reality of
the double baptism of Jesus: the baptism which he received
in the Jordan and which made him known as the well-
beloved Son of God, as well as the baptism he underwent
in the agony of his death and the joy of his resurrected life.

And for us, too, this will not be our last baptism. For as
disciples of Jesus we must steadfastly look for a second
baptism, a baptism in the Holy Spirit and in fire to which
we look forward with eagerness. It is a baptism which will
complete the encounter with Jesus and the knowledge of
him, deepen the reality of his presence and finally graft us
forever on to his death and resurrection. So we, too, live
between two baptisms. In the first we have already received
the fullness of Christ in principle. It is like a seed which
will soon demand the whole life of the believer in order later
to let all its hidden power unfold. It is like a fire which is
only a spark at first and then quietly begins to smoulder and
finally, especially through testings and affliction, breaks out
in flames for good and consumes everything it touches. It is
a fire like the Holy Spirit himself, who ignites in us the fire
of his love and consumes everything which cannot be made
into building material for his love. It is a fire which makes

us malleable and enables us to become one with that God of whom Scripture says that he is a consuming fire.

This is the fire which Jesus came to bring on earth, the fire of baptism in the Holy Spirit. It is also the baptism of Jesus which he still had to undergo in his death and resurrection and concerning which he now fervently wishes that it will be completed in each one of us (Luke 12:49–50).

9

The Money Wall

Like every one of us, Jesus also had to deal with money. First of all, he needed it to live and so he agreed to accept money from a group of well-to-do women who followed him everywhere. He also distributed alms through the agency of Judas who was appointed administrator. Once he was even willing to perform a miracle to pay a tax to the emperor. In his eyes, therefore, money was certainly not simply another word for sin.

But like us, Jesus also became acquainted with the relative value of money. He noticed immediately that the two small coins of the poor widow were of infinitely greater value than the jingling large coins of certain rich people. In fulfilling his task he also, in a sense, bumped into the money wall. This can be seen in the wall between him and the rich young ruler when he called the latter to follow him unconditionally. And in the end Jesus was also destroyed by money. He became the victim of the covetousness of one of his disciples, betrayed for thirty pieces of silver by one whose job it was to manage the disciples' money.

Of this essential ambiguity of money, Jesus would have had both good and bad memories, memories which resurface in the story of the dishonest steward (Luke 16:1–13). By decreasing the amounts owed by his master's debtors, the steward – who, despite this, was praised by Jesus – assured himself of their goodwill for the time when he would fall into disfavour. He did, of course, commit fraud by this action and thus proved himself even more dishonest. In no way could the problematic nature of money be better illustrated. Jesus, for that matter, speaks of 'the unrighteous mammon', dishonest wealth. And when he nevertheless praises the crooked manager, when he nevertheless commends this son of darkness to the children of light, he does it exclusively because the parable refers to a different kind of wealth, the wealth of heaven. The parable is intended to console the poor: 'I tell you, make friends for yourselves by means of dishonest wealth so that when it is gone, they may welcome you to the eternal homes' (Luke 16:9).

In Jesus' eyes there exists only one possibility for restoring money to its intended purpose: it has to be shared. He is especially hard on those who have become servants, even slaves, of money, on those who accumulate money for themselves alone. He had already often seen it happen that money became a wall between God and people. 'No one can serve two masters; for a slave will either hate the one and love the other, or be devoted to the one and despise the other. You cannot serve God and mammon' (Matt. 6:24). Sooner or later we will have to make a choice so that money may be made fruitful for God and for eternal life: 'Sell your possessions, and give alms. Make purses for yourselves that do not wear out, an unfailing treasure in heaven, where no thief comes near and no moth destroys.' Then Jesus adds: 'For where your treasure is, there your heart will be also' (Luke 12:33, 34).

This last statement cancels out the painful ambiguity attached to money. The most important thing, around which everything else ultimately revolves, is the heart: 'For where your treasure is, there your heart will be also.' It is as if Jesus is asking us: 'Where is your true treasure? And where, accordingly, is your heart? What, in truth, have you opted for? And if you think you have opted for me, how far does that choice go?'

It is therefore not surprising that Jesus declares the relinquishment of possessions as the condition of true discipleship. Sooner or later he will ask us to share our material and spiritual possessions in one form or another, solely out of love for him and because we want to be his disciple. For apart from him we possess no other treasure.

10

Giving from One's Poverty

Jesus was elated over the poor widow who offered two copper coins. She gave from her poverty and in so doing offered up everything she had to live on (Mark 12:42–4).

The others had also given money, a lot of it even, but 'from their surplus wealth'. Jesus had seen them all pass by the 'treasury' as each one deposited his gift. Many rich and generous people had put in large sums. Was it not right, then, for them to be so generous? Did Jesus perhaps want to reprimand them when he praised the poor widow? Absolutely not. Their gift, too, was welcome. All the money that was put in the treasury at the temple entrance would be used for the maintenance of the sanctuary. The scribes and Pharisees wanted to congratulate the generous donors and were grateful to them. And who knows, perhaps Jesus was too! They, after all, had done a good thing and would some day be rewarded for it as well.

Jesus, however, preferred the two miserable coins of the widow to these substantial gifts even though the coins were of no significance in the sum total of the collection. Why did he rate this gift more highly? Jesus' answer was very simple: 'She, from her poverty, put in everything she had, all she had to live on.'

Does this mean the others should have been more generous? Should they have given larger sums? Of course not. They were naturally free to do this and a higher contribution would certainly have been appreciated. But that was not what was important to Jesus; the issue was not so much one of quantity. Even if the rich were to give more, they would still only be giving from their abundance. For them it would always remain immensely difficult to give from their poverty. It is the same for us: whatever we may give of all the things that belong to us – our money, our time, our magnanimity, our health, our thousand good qualities – even if we put all this at Jesus' disposal, still we are only giving from our abundance. And it will always remain hard and even painful for us to give from our poverty.

To give everything to Jesus always means to give from our poverty and that is not an easy thing to do. But it is precisely this gift that Jesus expects from us all, the rich as well as the poor. Even the richest person among us – whether we are speaking of material or spiritual goods – must always give his poverty to Jesus and this is not easy. Jesus has already warned us about this very thing: it is hard for a rich person to enter the Kingdom. But even if it is impossible for human beings, for God all things are possible.

To give from our poverty means, first of all, to know that we are poor, that we have discovered in ourselves the wound for which (for that matter) no one is responsible but which for ever makes us utterly poor indeed, poor to a degree we would not dare to admit to ourselves. To give from one's poverty does not mean to gloss it over or to refuse to see it, not to secretly try to stash it behind the treasures of devotion or magnanimity which we can so freely display around ourselves. How easy that is, after all, for the rich person who is so lucky that he can give from his abundance. He may also easily conceal this poverty from himself and even be sincerely grateful because he is not like others. Let it be said again: a generous donation is neither inappropriate nor useless, quite the contrary is the case; but this does not release us from giving the only gift Jesus really expects from us – the gift of the two coppers of our poverty.

Happy, then, is this poor widow who is so poor that she has no excuse left with which to play hide-and-seek with grace. All that was left to her was her poverty, so she could only give these two paltry coins. Would she die of embarrassment? But why should she be ashamed? She accepts the fact that she just wants to give what she has because Jesus looked at her and accepted her as she was. Happy are they who dare to give from their poverty: in the eyes of Jesus they have given everything they had.

11

Our Final Wound

The gospel frequently highlights something remarkable in Jesus' conduct, as for example his way of dealing with the sick. Thus we read: 'He makes the deaf to hear and the mute to speak.' And this witness concerning Jesus is summed up in a telling and commendatory statement: 'He has done everything well' (Mark 7:31–7). Gradually Jesus would win the heart of the crowd, for in everything he did and said he was so different and always so competent. He succeeded in fascinating everybody. Little by little people would begin to speculate about why he came and, especially, who he was.

'He has done everything well.' This is how it was from the very first moment Jesus came into the world. By assuming a human body he came into contact with our earthly reality. From that moment on, even though no one could explain it, he was mysteriously different and powerful. There lodged within him a power he did not get from his parents but from the Holy Spirit by whom he was conceived. Later, from the time of his baptism in the Jordan and during his entire public ministry, this power, as the gospel puts it, began 'to come upon him to heal them all' (Luke 5:17). Did he know this and did he want it? Often one gets the impression that Jesus, as it were, allowed these miracles to slip from his healing body. In the beginning, at least, as in the case of the healing of the deaf man, Jesus did not want people to trumpet the news of this power to everyone. On the contrary, he expressly commanded the witnesses to talk to no one about it.

This mysterious power is something that would never leave Jesus. It would stay with him right up to the hour of his death throes, his final ordeal on the cross. For he had come for this ultimate ordeal, and through his death on the cross this mysterious power would ultimately triumph for good and cause him to rise from the dead. 'He has done everything well; he even makes the deaf to hear and the mute to speak.' Moreover, today he still does it for each of us. We might even add: 'He makes the blind to see again, the lame to walk, and raises the dead to life.' Today and always that selfsame power of Jesus dwells in the Church and effectively manifests itself in those who believe.

In one way or another many of us have already become acquainted with it. On a given day we too were called by this power which Jesus continues to exert and one of our hurts, too, was suddenly – unexpectedly and inexplicably – healed. The injury is not always physical; more frequently it is an inner or spiritual injury. Melancholy and bitter feelings or vague and undefinable disappointments sometimes suddenly vanish and seem to melt like snow before the sun by the touch of Jesus' hand or by his Word. And that, then, is only a beginning. For injuries will presumably always be there, one still only barely healed before another much deeper injury announces its presence. Even if the injuries keep accumulating, Jesus the physician will always be there and will continue to open the eyes and ears of our heart so that we, too, may not cease to see his marvellous acts of healing.

These ever-recurrent injuries, which are accompanied by as many healings, will end only at the time of our death, just as in the case of Jesus. They will end when all that belongs to Jesus' Easter has been fulfilled. Thus we will always be marked by some inner injury which to that degree is part of the fabric of our existence and which at the same time is so far from our consciousness that even our most intimate friends do not have an inkling of it; an injury so inextricably part of us that only death – the Easter of the Lord – will heal us of it. This is the injury which keeps us from seeing Jesus, at least for a time, for once endured, tended, healed, resurrected, this continuing injury will enable us to touch Jesus, to behold him, and for all eternity to sing of his mercy. For indeed, he has done everything well: he even makes the deaf to hear and the mute to speak.

12

Jesus' Icon in My Heart

After the feast of Easter Jesus held a place of ever-increasing importance in the life of his disciples. 'Believe in God,' he said to them, 'but believe also in me.' For from this point on, for those who believe in him and have taken it upon themselves to follow him, there is no other way of escape than Jesus. He is at the point of leaving his disciples but will return to bring them to where his Father is, so that they also may be where he is. Jesus' disciples have no other prospect left than Jesus, no other future than to be with him (John 14:1–12).

It is true: to attain the goal of being with God there is absolutely no other way than Jesus: 'No one comes to the Father except by me.' Jesus, accordingly, is their true life and their truth, a truth they can only receive from him. This process is the fulfilment, confirmation and perpetuation of their deepest existence. And there is more: they can only reach the Father, about whom Jesus was always talking and to whom he taught them to pray, in and through Jesus. The Father is not only in heaven, somewhere remote and hard to reach; he is very close. He becomes visible, tangible and completely accessible in Jesus. Just listen to the poignant question posed by Philip: 'Lord, show us the Father, and we will be satisfied.' Then follows the highly surprising and touching answer of Jesus. 'Whoever has seen me has seen the Father. How can you say: "Show us the Father"?

Do you not believe that I am in the Father and the Father is in me?'

These are indeed self-assured and moving words, words which Jesus also addresses to us. For right up to today the most important activity of the Church consists in looking at the face of Jesus and seeking in him the face of the Father: 'whoever sees me sees the Father'. Even though Jesus' physical face was visible on earth for only thirty-three years, yet in the Spirit, as St Paul puts it, it will always be present among us, ever within reach, to be seen and beheld by us.

That face is present, first of all, in the word of the gospel which confronts us with Jesus' doings and dealings. It is visible also in the Church, particularly when it assembles to celebrate the liturgy. We can also contemplate the divine countenance in the icons which in each separate case again show us another trait or feature of Jesus. It also directly manifests itself in each of our brothers and sisters: in him who is clothed with ecclesiastical authority and who occupies the place of Jesus, but also, perhaps especially, in the poorest persons among us, in the guest and in the stranger. Nothing more closely resembles the face of Jesus and of God than the face of a human being, from the most famous to the most miserable.

Of course, we must also be able to recognise it and that is not always simple. Each of the four gospels has its own view of Jesus. Our liturgy is sometimes diverse as well. The face of Jesus on our icons varies, depending on the time and region of their origin. In addition, as a result of their culture, race or skin colour, our brothers and sisters greatly differ from each other. How then can we recognise and contemplate the face of Jesus through all this diversity?

We would never succeed in this except for one thing: there is the divine iconographer, the Holy Spirit, who from the moment of our baptism, day after day, resculpts in our heart the features of Jesus' face, not only his physical face but also his 'spiritual' face. Every believer bears the glorious features of Jesus' face, the holy face of our beloved Saviour, as though it were engraved in his or her heart, usually – sadly enough – without knowing it. This spiritual face is one of the most precious things in existence, for simply from this interior face we can recognise Jesus wherever he shows himself. Therefore we can see how important is the diversity of facial features, of colour and style, language and liturgy, if by all these the Holy Spirit over and over reveals the eternal face of Jesus and his Father: 'Have I been with you all this time, Philip, and you still do not know me? Whoever has seen me has seen the Father.' (John 14:9)

13

No Law; Only Jesus Heals

We can approach the Word of God and the message of Jesus in two ways: from the outside or from the inside, with the intellect or with the heart. The Pharisees and scribes were familiar with the first approach and therefore continually sought to lure Jesus into a trap. Jesus, however, chose the second approach, an approach which could foil all their traps.

The Pharisees, though they sincerely attempted to glorify God, did this by blindly keeping the requirements and commandments of the Law and multiplying them to the nth degree. Hence in all the circumstances of life they knew exactly what they had to do or could not do. If, then, they scrupulously lived according to the Law they were sure that God was on their side, since they kept his Law. They also claimed the right to reprimand others who did not live according to the Law: people like Jesus and his disciples, for example, who dared to violate the extremely complex ritual which the Jews had built around every meal.

But Jesus disagreed: 'This people honours me with their lips,' he said with a quote from Isaiah, 'but their hearts are far from me' (Mark 7:6). What is the point of all these practices and customs? To get a grip on God? But suppose this is precisely the way God loses his grip on them? In order, despite everything, to gain power over God? Or very simply – and this is what Jesus suggested was going on – to avoid having any longer to take a good look at their own heart? Is it so that they can justify themselves to the outside world by their good behaviour and block out all the vague desires which were proliferating in their heart? But is a law imposed from without able to make the inmost heart healthy again?

Jesus did not even want to consider this possibility for the good reason that he had no fear whatever of the proliferating desires the human heart harbours. He quietly listed them: fornication, theft, murder, adultery, avarice, wickedness, deceit, licentiousness, envy, slander, pride, frivolousness. The list could not be worse or more terrifying. And Jesus added that all these things are present in the heart of every human being and their presence defiles a person. Not a single external requirement, however wise, necessary or compelling, can do a thing to change the situation and so purify or radically heal a person.

Only Jesus can do this. Precisely to that end did he come, not for all the healthy who know all the requirements of the Law, but for the sick. Not for the righteous who hide behind their obedience to the Law, but for sinners. He did not come to seek irreproachable scribes but lost sheep. He came for those who want to be very close to him in their heart, inasmuch as they have accepted living without feelings of fear in their heart because Jesus himself lives there and nowhere else. He lives in that wounded, bleeding heart which he knows through and through and in which nothing can shock or disconcert him. He feels nothing of what seems so hideous to us and so improbable, and which seems so only because it had never yet been looked at with infinite love and respect.

That is the reason why Jesus came to us. Not a single law could ever do this in his place. With one word, one gesture, or one look of love he restores in us what seemed irreparable. And if we choose to accept that, our heart, with everything that goes on in it, will be near to him as he is always near to it.

14

The Risk of Fasting

After Jesus had fasted for forty days and forty nights he became hungry. No part of human existence could remain unknown to him who came to save and redeem us. Even today many people still suffer genuine hunger, but what is the connection between Jesus' hunger and the salvation of human beings, between our fasting and the Easter of the Lord?

If we in the West have ever experienced hunger, then surely it would have been a rare occurrence, and for most of us it was probably merely something functional. We do not know the real meaning of hunger, in fact, and so are free to opt for it. But why, then, should we opt for it?

Some of our motives for fasting do not have anything directly to do with Jesus. If we were ever – perhaps for medical reasons – put on a strict diet or if we fasted to stay in good physical shape and to boost our athletic prowess, then these were certainly legitimate reasons which need no further explanation.

But certain motives for fasting do have a connection with Jesus' Easter. That would be the case, for example, if we limited our food expenditure in order to be able to share food with the poor, or if we fasted out of solidarity – personally and along with so many other people in the world – in order to experience hunger. There is no doubt that, by fasting, Jesus too sought to share in the enormous suffering of humankind.

But all these reasons, however noble, do not explain the secret of Jesus' fasting. Jesus simply fasted because he wanted to, as the gospel clearly says. But why? Because hunger never comes alone; hunger usually touches us very deeply, not just physically but deep in our heart. Hunger in a sense wounds us; it undermines something in us which up to that moment had been inviolable. It causes a kind of vacuum, tears open an old wound, and even at times leads to dizziness. Precisely for that reason fasting and hunger can change something in us, can even bring about a genuine transformation.

Whatever is thus touched or kindled is not always honourable or satisfying. We observe this in the story of Jesus in the wilderness: it is precisely because he is under the pressure of hunger that temptations arise in Jesus' heart. It would even have been reckless of him to wish to fast in this fashion had he not been driven into the wilderness by the Holy Spirit himself for the purpose of being tested by the devil there. After all, in order to be able to test us the devil has to take advantage of our weaknesses, both our physical and spiritual weakness, the hunger which torments us and makes us afraid of losing our life.

For along with hunger other desires and temptations immediately surface as well, even in the case of Jesus: the seductive challenge of easy success, the desire for earthly fame, the hunger for power in this world, sensuality in all its forms. Fasting half opens the door we so often want to keep shut, even with a double lock. For immediately after the first hunger and the first desire, the other hunger and those other desires surface as well, desires which seek – with equal bitterness and equal power to disturb us – to take possession of our heart. No one ever fasts with impunity, not even Jesus.

However, Jesus had come for this very purpose. Not to crush all desires and temptations, nor to conquer them honourably. The contrary is true. He will voluntarily – but without adverse effects – endure them in order thus to reach the other shore of our desires: 'If I cross the ravine of death, I will fear no evil, for You are with me.' The other shore of our desires: that is, the secret stirrings of our indecision and our whims, that which is the most intimate part of ourselves, that which we are. 'As the deer longs for the running waters, so my soul longs for you, O God' (Ps. 42–3:1). This is our hunger and thirst for God. Just as this was true for Jesus, so our fasting even today risks opening the door to the excitement of the desires it threatens to unleash, a door which looks out on the other shore of our desires, not on their dark but on their light side: God within us; God who desires to be loved; God who hungers for us and we for him, passionately.

15

Jesus' Never-ending Prayer

We listen to Jesus praying as he addresses his Father. As Son of the Father, he opens his heart to him and confides to him all his wishes (John 17:11–19). Jesus here articulates a deeply lived prayer at the end of the Last Supper, the evening before his passion. John the Evangelist was present and the words of Jesus' prayer remained forever engraved upon his heart, the heart of a friend.

This is not the only time Jesus prayed. Here and there the gospels contain other reports of him praying: Jesus who rejoiced in the spirit before his Father (Luke 10:21), who begs for his help or thanks him in advance for a miracle he is about to perform (John 11:41–2). It is certain that Jesus prayed much more than is reported in the gospels. The disciples have preserved the memory of those prayers as something that was very common: long evenings of prayer extending deep into the night. Jesus prayed very often, perhaps always! Could there have been a single moment in his earthly existence in which Jesus turned his gaze away from his Father, about whom he so confidently stated, 'The Father is always with me. The Father and I are one'?

Not even the suffering and death which awaited him would cut Jesus off from his Father. This death, remember, is his Father's will. Jesus identifies with this will; it is fulfilled in him. This death is the cup which his Father gives him to drink. This death will be realised in a cry and a sigh which is his last prayer: 'Father, into your hands I commend my spirit' (Luke 23:46). Jesus was to die praying.

Furthermore he will be praying when he arises as the First-born of the new creation. His adoring eyes will remain fixed on his Father, whose words for the last time he will once more hear: 'You are my beloved Son. Today I have begotten you.'

And he does not only arise praying. He also arises in order to pray, and to pray forever. The author of the letter to the Hebrews emphatically asserts this: ' . . . he always lives to make intercession for us' (Heb. 7:25). The high-priestly prayer which Jesus our high priest addressed to his Father and of which the evangelist handed down to us but a brief extract only began here on earth. It had to be continued forever. This ongoing prayer is the most important thing in the world, the only thing in the entire universe that carries real weight. It is the prayer of a human being who is God, this God who became human but who returned to his Father to present the universe to him for all eternity. On this prayer of Jesus the entire creation, the world with its history, the whole of humanity and the Church, remains dependent. Everything that lives and exists attains to its full development thanks solely to Jesus' prayer. Nothing can escape its reach. It is, irreversibly, the only way, the only door, the only mode of access. 'No one comes to the Father except by Me,' Jesus affirms.

Neither can anyone pray to the Father except by way of the prayer of Jesus. The ways of prayer are, and always have been, unfathomable. Throughout the course of history huge numbers of people have tried to pray, many of them exhausting all the means they thought they could trust. But who would dare say they actually reached the goal? Only the few who amidst so many efforts, and often thanks to so much effort, yet always apart from their striving, gave up all pretence of reaching this goal in their own strength. These few were suddenly seized by another power, which came from elsewhere and in place of their own strength; they were seized by another prayer, the only prayer that can penetrate into heaven in order finally to reach the Father, the only prayer also which will be completely and always heard: the prayer of Jesus himself, as well as every human prayer which is offered 'in Jesus' name'. 'Then the Father will give you everything you ask him.'

In the core of our liturgy the miracle can be realised – each time anew – on behalf of the poor among us, who humbly and confidently put their faith in the one prayer of Jesus. Did he not promise us, 'Anyone who comes to me I will never drive away'?

16

Jesus: My Father and My Mother

Who is Jesus? This question, a question which every one of us will pose sooner or later, is answered in the gospel by Jesus himself: 'I am your shepherd, the only good shepherd, your only true shepherd' (John 10:11–18). For there are shepherds – and shepherds! This comparison, one which Jesus derives from the Old Testament, remains ambiguous if one thinks of earthly shepherds. Accordingly, it must be interpreted. There are shepherds, after all, who only work for wages: they attach much more importance to their wages than to the sheep. There is no bond between them and the sheep; they barely know one another. The moment the wolf appears on the scene such shepherds take off, leaving the sheep in the lurch. 'He is only a hired hand and has no heart for the sheep,' says Jesus (John 10:13).

The relation between Jesus and his sheep is very different. The bond which has grown between him and the sheep has nothing to do with money or wages: it is a bond of blood. He gave his life for his sheep. It is by his death that Jesus acquired his sheep; it is by his death that we were born of him. It was a death powered by love, hence a love that was stronger than death.

It was a death which produced a birth. The shepherd's death was simultaneously the gift and the resumption of life. 'I lay down my life in order to take it up again,' he says. 'I have power to lay it down and I have power to take it up again' (John 10:17–18). Jesus gave his life for his sheep but resumed it to be able to share it with his sheep. This death, which was born of love, becomes a wellspring of life; it gives birth; it is maternal. All of us, and also the Church, were born from this death, from the wound in the side of the crucified Shepherd. Therefore, however strange this may seem, Jesus the Shepherd mainly has the traits of a mother, a mother who was prepared to lay down her life in order to bring us into the world.

For that reason Jesus also knows us as only a mother can. 'I know my sheep and my sheep know me' (John 10:14). Therefore we also know Jesus as only a child can know and sense his mother. A child born from her womb, born of her pain, will always remember that his mother loved him to the point of death.

This maternal bond between Jesus and his sheep is so close that he reminds us of another bond, one that is even more intense: 'Just as the Father knows me and I know the Father, so I know my sheep and my sheep know me' (John 10:14-15). Here we face a mystery which completely baffles us, even though in certain blissful moments we experience something of a strange similarity, something of the bond which exists between Jesus and each one of us: 'Just as the Father has loved me.' Jesus the Word was also born from all eternity, begotten in the bosom of the Father. Jesus was born, not from a real death – how could death exist in God? – but from a Father who completely emptied himself, who essentially communicated himself to his Word (says theology), who is the perfect image of himself, who does not cease to give back to him all the love he received from him. 'For this reason the Father loves me, because I lay down my life.' The Son loves the Father because he received life from him.

Who, then, is Jesus to me? My only true Shepherd with

whom not a single earthly shepherd can be compared, to whom no mother or father can be compared. Who is Jesus to me? The Mother above all mothers, in comparison with whom all motherliness on earth shrinks into nothing. Who is Jesus for me? The Father above all fathers, from whom all fatherhood on earth takes its name. Who is he? A friend, a spouse, a love which will ultimately never know its equal because he gave his life for those he loved.

17

A Time for Love

At the creation of the world and humanity God also instituted time. Time is not necessary to God but it is to humans who need time to live and to assign the right measure to all things. It is needed first of all for us to be born. A full-term baby lives peacefully ensconced in its mother's womb for nine months. Once born, after a time it will begin to laugh; a short while later it takes its first uncertain little steps. Again, it will be a while before the baby can mouth its first real words. So, while every stage has its own discoveries, it will be several years before the child can stand on his own two feet, before he can love someone other than his parents.

It will especially take a long time for a human being to learn to love. And to deepen the love one has chosen once-and-for-all requires much longer. Many years of faithfulness await a person; it is a lifelong enterprise. Time, after all, was especially given for love, for the love between humans as well as for the love between a human being and God. To learn to love calls for an enormous amount of time. Because people are so fickle and because God so often remains hidden and totally beyond our reach, time will in fact prove to be the only idiom in which humans can express their love. Time, accordingly, is intended to become a language of love.

In the parable Jesus tells about the foolish and the wise bridesmaids God plays with time in an extremely refined and nimble way (Matt. 25:1–13). The wedding which is central to this parable is that of God's Son and the Church, the wedding between Jesus and every believer. Through Jesus, God himself entered into human time at a specific moment of our history which would be once and for ever marked by it. Jesus, nevertheless, only lived on earth for a short time, for the duration of a human life. He came and went, but what is especially important is that he is coming back. And the time still remaining only serves for us to look forward to his return. Time now is completely controlled by Jesus' second coming. The Church similarly keenly looks forward to his coming; its very life consists in nothing other than confident, patient, passionate waiting until he comes.

Hence for every one of us, from now on, time is exclusively devoted to love; it is a matter of watching in love. This is also the only thing that was expected of the bridesmaids in the parable and those invited to Jesus' wedding. All that was required was to wait and be ready. For, as Jesus said, the bridegroom kept people waiting. This does not seem strange to us because Jesus also keeps us waiting. That is precisely the divine element in God's game with human time, the time which all love on earth needs to truly reveal itself. A love which is merely like a flash of lightning can flare up high but time – waiting and patient watching – will bring about a depth which goes beyond feelings. This is a depth that will one day end in a wedding feast which is now still inconceivable, and Jesus himself will be waiting for us at the door.

When the waiting takes long, it becomes a test, certainly, but also a challenge. For the long wait is intended to bring about the decisive division between those who love and those who vacillate in love. The bridesmaids did not all react to the continued absence of the bridegroom in the same way.

When he came, some of them had the needed extra oil at their disposal and the others did not. The former were allowed to enter the banquet hall; the latter were not. Jesus did not stop to explain to us the symbolism of this oil, but we can guess that it has something to do with love and expectation. As a result of the boredom of the long wait some began to doubt and were ultimately no longer recognised by Jesus. During the same long wait and the same boredom others continued to believe in Jesus' love. And their faith stirred his heart. Their faith in love meant their salvation.

18

Weak and Strong, with Jesus

'I will strike the shepherd and the sheep will be scattered.' With these words from the prophet Zechariah (13:7) Jesus announces the events which are about to happen. The shepherd and the sheep are part of the same scenario. The path of the shepherd will be that of the sheep also, because, like the sheep, the shepherd does not want to be spared. And the disciples will go the way of the Master because the Master, as the first to do so, has chosen to share the fate of the disciples. The shepherd and the sheep, the Master and his followers, Jesus and ourselves, all are united on the threshold of the suffering of Easter in which we will become real participants.

And this is true from the first scene, the scene enacted in the Garden of Gethsemane. Peter, James and John are not present just as witnesses of the struggle waged by Jesus: they are fellow actors in his drama, each in his own way and on his own level. And this, it seems, is also what Jesus expected from their presence: 'Simon, could you not stay awake with me one hour?'

The death-struggle Jesus experienced in Gethsemane is the death-struggle of all humanity, which, like Jesus, has to face the same inner conflict that he summed up by saying, 'The spirit is willing but the flesh is weak'. Jesus is spared none of this weakness just as we will be spared none of it: Jesus 'began to be grieved and agitated. He said to them: "I am deeply grieved, even to death . . ." He threw himself on the ground and prayed that, if possible, this hour might pass him by. "Abba, Father, all things are possible to you. Let this cup pass me by".' (Mark 14:33–6) How enormous the weakness which can threaten the flesh! At certain moments it can seem lethal and quenches, as it were, all the fire of the Spirit.

While at the same moment the disciples lived through this weakness of Jesus in the hour of his temptation, there was a difference: they simply succumbed to it. True, their trial was not as decisive as that of Jesus, for their hour had not yet come. Jesus had asked them to stay awake with him. But it was not long before they fell asleep, 'for their eyes were heavy' with fatigue. Even though their spirit wanted to be strong – only a short time earlier Peter had been talking about his unbreakable loyalty to Jesus – the flesh was terribly weak.

However, Jesus had proposed to them a good method – a battle plan you could call it – needed to ensure victory. 'Stay awake and pray that you may not enter into the trial.' And he himself provided the model. For the immense weakness of the flesh, for Jesus as well as for us, is always counterbalanced by the enormous power of the Spirit: watching and praying are the pre-eminent means by which we may endure human weakness without losing solid ground beneath our feet.

In Gethsemane, where the most treacherous of all temptations could have been fatal for him, Jesus held his own and, in and through prayer, learned obedience to the Father. He succumbed to the power and sweetness of the Father's love: 'Not what I want, Father, but what you want.' Given this love, what does it matter that the flesh continues to be so terribly weak when, like Jesus, we can over and over again yield ourselves to prayer and the power of the Spirit.

19

Clothed in Weakness

Everything started for Jesus with a forty-day period in the wilderness, ending with the temptations. Before he could announce the nearness of the Kingdom, before he could disclose the road which would take him to Jerusalem and to his Easter, there was this time of trial face-to-face and eye-to-eye with Satan.

An impossible assignment. It would seem on the face of it that this was not what Jesus wanted but he could not escape from it. Since at his baptism the Spirit had come upon him, Jesus lived totally under his spell: 'the Spirit drove him into the wilderness', as the evangelist notes (Matt. 4:1), to enter the ring against the adversary.

Even though Jesus himself did not choose this detour by way of the wilderness, a few years later, the author of the letter to the Hebrews was to see the absolute necessity of it. This was the purpose for which Jesus had come, this author wrote. 'He himself was tested in every respect, as we are, yet without sin' (Heb. 4:15). Thus he explored the dizzying weakness of humans, experienced it in body and soul, to become a high priest who understands and empathises and is capable of curing it. 'Clothed in weakness,' writes the same author (5:2), referring to our human weakness which Jesus wore as a priestly garment and in which he led the way to bring his Easter sacrifice.

And it was 'clothed in weakness' that Jesus also went out to meet the temptations in the wilderness. And so it had to be for his temptation to be genuine and not make-believe. Jesus had to be besieged by the infatuation of the desires and stagger, as it were, under the impact of their seductive gravitational pull. All the details of these temptations, which we can recognise without any trouble, have been preserved by the evangelists. As Jesus wandered in the wilderness, the hunger for food, the desire for power and the pursuit of fame, ravaged his heart and in some hallucinatory way became reality, just as these same temptations also tear up our hearts and strive to seduce them with false promises.

No one can expose himself to such temptations with impunity, not even Jesus. The weakness of his human body, the body he shares with us, would – if left to itself – have succumbed, just as we succumb. But the Spirit led him through this trial. From the time of his baptism, when he heard the voice of his Father from above, Jesus was never totally alone again: his Father was always by his side, even at the lowest point of the temptation. And the power of God was to grow to its full point of development in his human weakness. By withstanding the temptation in this fashion and by overcoming it in the power of the Spirit, Jesus opened a road by which every one of us can now follow him through our own trials and weakness.

None of us will be spared this experience, nor the harrowing experience of dizzying weakness. Just as Jesus reeled under the impact of the temptations, so we, too, will be threatened by them. Just as he was tested, so we on our part will have to endure temptations. But there is no other way to be saved. Fortunately Jesus opened that road for us.

For from here on, however paradoxical it may sound, every temptation and every human weakness will be accompanied by the power of Jesus. It is like seed which he himself planted at the moment when he, as the first, struggled through the trial in our name and for us all. All temptations and every weakness now bear within them the grace of the Lord Jesus. They are a possible sacrament of his Easter victory, provided we never let ourselves become discouraged and firmly continue to believe in him, calling on his Name without ceasing and allowing ourselves to be formed and led by the gentleness of his Spirit.

20

Fear and Shame

'All who do evil hate the light and do not come to the light because they are afraid' (see John 3:16–21). These words of Jesus recall for us the ancient story of Adam and Eve after the fall. When God walked in the garden at the time of the evening breeze they were so ashamed and afraid they went and hid themselves (Gen. 3:8). They knew they were naked and humans do not enter the light naked. They seek their salvation in concealment, choosing the darkness over the light.

The entire history of humankind, in fact, is marked by this shame and dread before God, from the first sin committed by Adam, through the countless sins committed by all people since, right up until the coming of Jesus. All sinners try to hide out of fear that they will be recognised and condemned. But through Jesus, and thanks to his Easter, everything became thoroughly different; the endlessly long history of shame came to an end. The evangelist John tries to make this reversal clear with a word play that is peculiar to him and which, at the time he is writing, in the period in which the definitive redaction of the New Testament came into being, is the fruit of a long and perhaps even a sad reflection on the scandal and dishonour of Jesus' death on the cross. St John's language plays with the double meaning of the verb 'to lift up'. Jesus was lifted up on the cross. he writes, but precisely this elevation into dishonour was also an elevation into glory. For he was lifted up on the tree of the cross – like the brass serpent in the wilderness – to bring healing and salvation to all who turn to him and cast a believing and salvific look at him.

In Jesus, the Jesus who was lifted up on the cross, everything will henceforth be different. Jesus took upon himself the shame and the fear our father Adam felt because he was naked by letting himself be nailed naked to the shameful tree of the cross. And the doom pronounced on the sinner Adam was assumed by Jesus in accepting death on the cross, for, as it was written in the Law, 'Cursed is everyone who hangs on a tree' (Gal. 3:13). By taking upon himself all the shame of the nakedness and sin in Adam's, and in our, place, Jesus once and for all brought it before the merciful eyes of his Father. For to that end did he come. God so loved the world that he sent his only Son, not to condemn the world, but so that the world should be saved by him. Hence it is out of mercy that we are saved.

And from this point on sinners should no longer hide; they have been reprieved from disgrace. So let them come to the light, more specifically to the light of Jesus' cross. For to the nakedness of Jesus, the only Son, a nakedness which is graced and restored, our own nakedness and sinfulness no longer has a reason for embarrassment or condemnation. It has become an opportunity for faith, faith that can arise even from a foolish self-confidence. Just as it was for the Israelites who were mortally bitten by snakes in the wilderness, so for sinners now it is enough to raise themselves up and, full of faith, look up to our 'serpent', to Jesus, lifted up on the shameful tree of the cross, which is henceforth transformed into a cross of honour and salvation.

It is enough to look, but we must really look. For from now on we will be saved only by such a look at Jesus and by his grace. Only those who believe in Jesus will not perish but escape judgement and already possess eternal life now. But those who do not want to believe are already condemned because they have no confidence; because, as in the case of Adam and Eve, they are too deeply consumed by shame and fear. They lack the courage humbly and gently to turn their gaze toward the bleeding face of the crucified Jesus – and only toward him – to direct their gaze toward the shame of Jesus who covers and hides ours; especially toward his love, a love which could not be any greater because he gave his life. By such a grace we are saved, for thus Jesus loved us and gave himself up for us all.

21

A Stroke of Grace

In the village of Nazareth in Galilee the girl Mary, the recipient of a sensational message from the angel Gabriel, was not a striking figure. She was even astonished and afraid. She did not understand much of it and raised questions because she didn't know what had happened to her. She was really not an arresting, eye-catching young woman. Why, then, did the Lord's eye fall upon her among so many others?

Why? The greeting the angel used when he entered the room where Mary was suggests an initial answer. He called her 'full of grace', 'favoured', for, he said, she 'had found favour with God' (Luke 1:30). Her election by God over all others was an act of pure grace and gratuity. It was an act of love and love cannot be explained. Love just happens and, what's more, happens exclusively by means of things which are inexplicable. If love could be explained, it would no longer be love, not even in the eyes of God. That, after all, is the law of love among humans and in speaking to them even God cannot escape that law. It is as if God himself cannot explain the reasons for his choice and this is no different, for that matter, from when we speak of a beating heart, a flash of lightning, a stroke of grace. When Mary then began to reflect on this divine election, she offered us a second answer. By choosing her, she says, he has cast his eye on the humility and lowliness of his maidservant (Luke 1:48). Thus we learn that Mary saw her own adventure along

[60]

the lines of salvation history as a whole and of the Psalms. God always remains true to himself: he always gives himself to the little ones; he is always on the side of the humble and hears the prayers of the poor. Littleness and lowliness exert an irresistible attraction for him. They, as it were, constitute a prey to his infinite love. He has no choice, given his character, but to praise the humble. From all eternity this was the sign of his mercy as he showed it to our fathers from generation to generation. Hence Mary, the young girl, was not consulted in connection with the miracle which came over her.

But that is not the whole truth: in a way she was consulted. God did not wish to force her; he could not use violence; he could not simply confront her with a *fait accompli*. That, to him, would be the opposite of love. He awaited her affirmation – even begged for it – for in love the consent of the other party is essential, absolutely necessary. In total freedom Mary answered: 'Let it happen to me according to your word!' Perhaps this does not seem unusual but it is nevertheless full of meaning, for without this free response God's upsurge of love would have remained forever fruitless and without effect.

We all of us and the Church as a whole also continually have a chance to say yes to grace, every day anew. For those who agree to grace will suddenly see miracles and marvels light up. As long as grace has not manifested itself before our eyes, we can only agree with ourselves, our own powers and projects, or with those of others, and as we wait we find there a wonderfully honest alibi with which God is satisfied for the time being. But when God's grace finally manifests itself in our heart, everything becomes infinitely simple. This is because grace simplifies everything. It gives us peace; it infallibly points out to us the place where we find ourselves

before God, to be and to do that to which we have been
called in the Kingdom. With its infinite gentleness it leads
us infallibly to our complete unfolding in God. To that end
we must always be like the little maidservant of the Lord
and say yes to grace and know, as Mary did, that we really
do not amount to much.

22

Getting Past the Law

Some aspects of Jesus' public ministry deeply offended the Jews, such as the enormous freedom he permitted himself with respect to the Law. Jesus did not observe the sabbath with the degree of meticulousness required by rabbinical practices. Nor did he fast as was considered proper, a matter in which his disciples often followed his example. This state of affairs could not go on indefinitely, for Jesus was bound to be asked for an explanation. His clarification is extremely important because it constitutes the core of the Good News (Matt. 5:17–37). It was of great importance in his own time and is still of great importance for us today.

From the beginning Jesus affirmed that he had come not to abolish the Law but, on the contrary, to fulfill it. But what does he mean by the fulfilment of the Law? Does it mean recovering the text from under layers of dust in order to apply it to a new situation? Creating greater clarity in the Law to make it applicable to all conceivable cases? Increasing the gravity of the Law by prescribing a range of heavy penalties for violating it? This is what every legislator would do if at some point he wanted to review and revise the Law. This, however, was not what Jesus had in mind. He did not come to clarify the Law or make it more rigorous. He had in mind a much more weighty goal: he wanted to radically change the law. What matters, says Jesus, is no longer the Law but *righteousness*, a word by which he means inner holiness: 'unless your righteousness exceeds that of the scribes and Pharisees, you will never enter the kingdom of heaven' (Matt. 5:20). St Paul even goes so far as to say that the Law no longer exists for those who are 'in Jesus Christ', that the letter of the Law 'kills' and only the Spirit 'gives life' (2 Cor. 3:6).

Was Jesus not the first to declare that his law and his commandment were completely new? Did he not say that this one commandment of love for God and his brothers would henceforth be the summary of the whole Law and the prophets?

But how can we make a choice between 'law' and 'love'? And above all, how can we rank 'love' higher than the 'law'? *We* who have so often injured and denied love and applied it to our own advantage, so that even love has become violent and unpredictable? Is not the law a necessary form of protection to shield love from all kinds of foolishness, to restrain its potential excesses? How can we ever say with St Augustine: 'Love and do what you want'?

However, even through the distant impression we have of our first steps in love not everything is completely mistaken. For one thing, there is the fact that love cannot be coerced; additionally, the moment we really begin to love, love prompts us joyfully to accept every law as an irresistible source, as if we have finally begun to exist, as if love has broken every barrier, as if henceforth all things are permissible.

In order correctly to evaluate these initial impressions (which, though not false, are incomplete), we must look at that same love from the other end of the road, when our first love has deepened, when our love for God, which is in our heart thanks to the Holy Spirit, will finally have turned into complete joy. Then for us and our love there will no longer be a law, because our law and our love will be one and our only love will be the Spirit of God.

Does this mean that a Christian is a person who loves without law? Indeed: but only in the sense that no single human law will still be sufficient for him or her, for the law of a Christian is that of God and nothing less than love itself. True love will always take a person infinitely further than any law is able to do.

Love springs up in us not only to position us above the law but ultimately to replace the law, and to do that by its own power, the Spirit of God. Only the Spirit is able infallibly and freely to lead us beyond the law and beyond ourselves to where God wants and expects us to be.

23

Love Is Immortal

In Jesus' day the Jews used to raise questions about life after death and specifically about whether the dead will arise. And, just as they are today, opinions were divided. So the Jews came to Jesus to interrogate him (Luke 20:27–38).

The question they asked him proved not to be too deep for him. On the issue of life after death he seemed supremely self-confident. In the blink of an eye he swept the objections of the Sadducees from the table. As to the woman who was successively married to seven different men, whose wife will she be in the hereafter? Answer: this other life will be totally different from the present life; we will neither marry, nor die, nor even be able to die. In everything we will be like the angels, children of God forever.

To that degree Jesus is content to confirm the resurrection, even though he offers no proof. But is the resurrection something that can be proved? Has anyone ever crossed the boundary of death and then returned? Apart from Jesus and Mary, no one ever rose from the dead, hence no one can witness to the reality of resurrection. But Jesus would suggest something that could serve as proof. 'God', he commented as he spoke about Moses and the burning bush, called himself 'the God of Abraham, the God of Isaac, and the God of Jacob'. God, therefore, is not a God of the dead but of the living, 'for to him all of them are alive', says Jesus.

What can we say about that? That proof for the resurrection lies in God himself and in the extraordinary bond he created between himself and people. God is absolute fullness of life, that is fullness of knowledge and love. This life he intended to share with humans to whom he gave himself in order to be known, to minister and to love. A creature so intimately connected with God – 'I am the God of Abraham, the God of Isaac, and the God of Jacob' – a creature who thus belongs to God, and God to him, cannot cease to exist. Such a creature shares in the fullness of life it has received from God; it participates in the love of God in which it can only live forever. God, after all, is a God of the living, not of the dead. Have not all received their life from him? The certainty of the resurrection is God himself, the God who gives it, the bond of love by which he unites us to him.

So it was already in the time of the patriarchs, even though the Jews were not conscious of it, and so it was in the time of Jesus even before he entered his Easter. But since that Easter there is much more. By the death and resurrection of a human who was God's own Son, he has furnished scintillating and definitive proof. For the person who lives in Christ, accordingly, for one with whom Jesus has united himself in a true bond of love which is permanent, for one who, with St Paul, can say every day: 'I live, yet it is no longer I who live but Christ who lives in me' (Gal. 2:20), doubt is no longer possible. Even if to the rational intellect the resurrection still has to be proved, even if it remains improbable – and why should it not? – the love-bond which unites a person to Jesus, acting from within, as it were, thrusts upon him or her proof of the opposite. It is Jesus himself, after all, who on a certain day will take us with him through death to eternal life. For where Jesus is, there also his disciple and friend will be.

For the friend of Jesus, then, everything will be different

from now on – not only life but also death. 'For to me, living is Christ and dying is gain,' said St Paul (Phil. 1:21). Whatever may happen, we belong to Jesus and Jesus belongs to us. Who can separate us from the love of God in Jesus Christ (see Rom. 8:35)? 'Neither death, nor life,' said the same apostle, nothing in this world or the next. For that matter, 'as long as we are alive, we live for the Lord, and if we die, we die to the Lord. So then whether we live or die, we are the Lord's' (Rom. 14:8). Therefore what is the difference between life and death? The Lord always goes ahead of us; he keeps us united to him; wherever he goes he takes us along with him. So, if his love for us is so great, it can only go on forever and ever.

24

Only Love Heals

Jesus and Zacchaeus, two persons who at first sight had nothing in common, met (Luke 19:1–10). Zacchaeus was a Jew who collaborated with the Roman occupation. He was the chief toll collector in the area and because of this universally detested occupation he was viewed as a despicable lost sheep, a traitor to his people. When Jesus appeared Zacchaeus was driven by a peculiar desire: 'He was trying to see who Jesus was' says the gospel. But because he was a small man, he was pushed aside by the crowd at every opportunity. Once, when Jesus again came through Jericho, Zacchaeus ran ahead of him and climbed into a sycamore tree. There he could keep an eye on Jesus without being hindered. An undefined curiosity was to afford him the chance of a lifetime.

But did Jesus also want to see Zacchaeus? The gospel does not tell us. From his perch in the branches of the sycamore tree Zacchaeus could not in any case escape Jesus' attention. He had stationed himself there, almost as a target. Jesus only needed to raise his eyes in order, whether he wanted to or not, to look straight into the eyes of Zacchaeus – and that's precisely what happened. Zacchaeus was used to seeing only faces which hardened when he passed by, eyes which turned away from him and shunned him. Only rarely did anyone give him a second look and then their eyes usually soon filled up with hatred and contempt. Thus in various subtle ways he was made to feel that he did not belong to the people of God.

Jesus' attitude and look were totally different. Jesus looked at Zacchaeus, stared at him even. At first Zacchaeus must have felt surprised and uneasy. Jesus' gaze was so different from the looks he encountered every day or had perhaps stopped seeing long ago because they hurt him so badly, even though he knew he deserved them. Jesus' eyes did not condemn or hurt him. They received, enveloped, warmed him; even more, they caressed him. Zacchaeus was as he was: a sad customer, a miserable traitor, right up until that moment. But the eyes of Jesus, like the eyes of his Father, made no distinction between the evil and the righteous. Zacchaeus had the right to be as he was: worse than a sinner, but no less loved by Jesus for all that.

An unexpected peace came over Zacchaeus, a deep sense of relief. What was actually happening here? He could barely believe his eyes but neither could he doubt Jesus' look. And the crowd could not believe this scene either; they were even more astonished than Zacchaeus. Now what? Was Jesus actually planning to speak to this rogue? Indeed: Jesus not only directed his gaze toward Zacchaeus but addressed him. He even called him by his first name as if he knew him from the past, as if he was not in the least surprised to find him in that location, here in the curve of the road, high up in the sycamore tree, as though he had come to Jericho for the sole purpose of seeing the chief toll collector.

There was still more. Jesus not only spoke to him but invited himself over to his house: 'Zacchaeus,' he said, 'hurry and come down for today I must be a guest in your home.' Suddenly the strange peace Zacchaeus had felt turned into overwhelming joy. Crazy with joy, he came tumbling down from his perch and hastened to honour Jesus with the request that he come to his, Zacchaeus', house. But Zacchaeus did not stop there. He went much further, deciding to give half of his possessions to the poor; that meant giving them to Jesus himself. Zacchaeus was beside himself. For him it was enough just once to be lovingly approached by Jesus' gaze and, on his part, to honour others with the same service of love.

Now the righteous and the Pharisees had full scope in which to be offended: 'He has gone to be the guest of one who is a sinner,' they muttered. Zacchaeus was a sinner indeed but to Jesus no less worth loving for all that: on the contrary, as is evident from Jesus' solemn statement: 'For the Son of Man came to seek out and to save the lost.' Against the injuries of sin there is, accordingly, but one remedy: the love of Jesus, which is always greater than our heart, and his grace, which is superabundant precisely where sin is so abundant.

25

God: Weak with the Weak

The Pharisee began his prayer very well: 'God, I thank you . . .' This was the familiar formula with which Jews usually began public or private prayer. Usually they were prayers of praise or thanksgiving (Luke 18:9–14). Once, when Jesus turned to his Father in the presence of his disciples, he used a similar formula: 'I thank you, Father, Lord of heaven and earth . . .' (Matt. 11:25).

But that's where the parallel ends. The objects of Jesus' thanksgiving, and of the Jews of his day, were the countless marvellous acts of God from the time of creation: the exodus from Egypt; the entry into the Promised Land; the return from exile; the entire course of salvation history. And as it concerns Jesus, there were more things: the miracles the Father performed through him, like the raising of Lazarus; his hiding the secrets of the Kingdom from the wise and intelligent and revealing them to the little ones.

But the Pharisee was not thinking of God but of himself. Though he gave thanks to God, it was not because of his marvellous deeds. He only thanked God for the miracle which he supposed *himself* to be and which he did not hesitate to proclaim out loud: he differs from the others, for he is better than they are; he is not a thief, not unjust; he does not commit adultery; and, above all, he is not a publican like the other fellow some distance behind him in the temple, whose reprehensible appearance alone offends him. He, by contrast, fasts and meticulously pays his tithes. Was this

Pharisee perhaps a mere boaster, somewhat more garrulous and naïve than others? His problem, unfortunately, lies much deeper. Luke offers a correct analysis: this Pharisee belongs to those who think themselves righteous, who feel self-assured and despise sinners. Or, as he puts it elsewhere, they were among those who had no need for mercy and therefore no need for God's marvellous deeds.

The situation of the publican was totally different. He had to gather up all his courage even to enter the temple. He felt excluded from society, distrusted and rejected by public opinion. Daily he had to deal with the scorn of the 'right-minded'; the prayer the Pharisee had just uttered in his presence with a deliberately loud and clear voice humiliated him to the core and pushed him more deeply into desperation. Against God and this so-called righteous man he could not do a thing. He was especially powerless to present anything positive to offset the negative, not even a minimally good deed, not the least bit of merit, nor could he claim any rights. There he stood, empty-handed, his heart full of despair. In the darkest corner of his despair there was only that one point of light: the mercy, the sweet compassion of God. That was what he begged for; to that he surrendered himself, despite his deep despair. And that was enough for him. He had nothing to fear. However deeply he may have fallen, stronger still is the humility and sweet compassion of God which he would – willingly or unwillingly – encounter some day.

It was his ardent trust in God's mercy which gave him a sense of relief, while the Pharisee was blocked by his self-sufficiency. In this way, even today, God's compassion accomplishes miracles. This is, from now on, the source of the only prayer that is valid, the only true Eucharist: thanksgiving which arises from an appeal to God's mercy, the astonishing weakness of God which is at the same time his only form of omnipotence and which is capable of doing wonders. 'I thank you, Father, Lord of heaven and earth, because you are gracious toward the sinner that is I.'

26

Deepening the Nature of Love

The parable of the lost son is a parable about joy: first the joy of the son who, after wasting all he had, became deliriously happy. Then there is the joy of the father who was initially deeply hurt but became altogether tender later. Finally, there is the joy of the older son who is a little too virtuous and does not know how much he, too, is loved. They are three very different personalities, all of whom will in the end experience a genuine deepening of love (Luke 15:11–32).

First let us consider the attitude of the father. He was a good and understanding father, whose goodness had never yet been tested and therefore had not yet become fruitful; that is, until his younger, more beloved son caused him the humiliation and pain of prematurely taking off with his part of the inheritance. It was an injury which would prove necessary to deepen his paternal love and allow it to flourish more vigorously than before. The longer the time of affliction and waiting lasted, the stronger his love became. Day after day, without ever giving up hope, he was on the lookout to see whether or not his son was approaching in the distance, his figure appearing over the horizon. The father was, after all, firmly convinced that his child would return, and that his love would gain the upper hand.

Then there was the attitude of the wastrel. Initially his father's love had aroused annoyance in him as he experienced an all-too-quiet life without problems or surprises. How can a person know he is being loved when nothing is happening? The rude departure was perhaps no more than an awkward challenge to his father: how far could he go and still remain assured of his father's love? But how utterly evanescent were the pleasures in the far country, pleasures which led to his degradation. Materially, morally and psychologically he very soon became a human wreck, so that he was no longer even considered worthy to share the fodder of the swine he was supposed to herd.

Though the son was not aware of it, the father patiently waited for him. How could he have known? He no longer had anything more than a completely unconscious bond with his father, a bond strong as death nevertheless, and vital as the life that springs from it, a bond which paternal love weaves between a father and the son who sprang from his loins. The son did not know it, even though it was the unremitting love of his father which from a distance still pierced his heart, enabled him to remain himself and nurtured in him the desire to go home again. This was the bond which inspired in him the words of humility which no love, however injured, could resist: 'Father, I have sinned against heaven and against you; I am no longer worthy to be called your son, but please take me on as one of your hired men.' A father's love cannot resist such words; neither, undoubtedly, can the love of God. When the father saw him coming from afar, he was moved to compassion, ran out to meet him, put his arms around him and showered him with kisses.

Finally there was the older son. Initially he did not understand the joy of a forgiveness which seemed all too easy; also, he was bitter and angry. So much undeserved mercy made him furious. He who had always been responsible and well-behaved, was he not the one who had a right to be rewarded? But alas, because he thought himself righteous, because he fancied he could make claims on his father's love, he no longer saw the extent to which he himself lived in grace and mercy. Because he no longer saw how much he himself continually needed mercy, he also no longer knew how much he was loved. The father gently chided him: 'Son, you are always with me, and all that is mine is yours.' The older son completely forgot his joy because he had never been dead and then become alive again, never been lost and then found again. How true it is that there is more joy in heaven and the Church over one sinner who returns than over ninety-nine righteous who have no need for repentance. There is no other joy than this divine tenderness which ever and again forgives us.

27

God on the Lookout!

The ideas Jesus and his discussion partners tossed back and forth are actually just a reflection of the things which still engage us today (Luke 13:1–9). Accidents happen or disasters strike and almost always there are victims. Then, almost inevitably, the question arises: were they guilty? And of what? Does God wreak vengeance upon them on account of their sins?

This is like an inborn reaction, fed by ancestral fears of which each of us presumably has his share, but which Jesus, when he was asked about them, most vigorously rejected. The God who becomes visible behind all those fears, a cruel and vengeful God, has, strictly speaking, nothing to do with the God whom Jesus came to make known, the God who is his own Father, the Father of all goodness and mercy.

Furthermore, we are not living in a situation in which on the one hand there are sinners whom God secretly seeks to catch in the act and on the other the righteous who have nothing to fear because they are 'all right' with God and therefore have no need of his mercy. On this point Jesus is very clear: the Galileans who were slain by Pilate and the unfortunates who were crushed under the falling stones of the tower of Siloam were not greater or lesser sinners than all other people. We are all sinners and all of us need mercy. Jesus strikes a very formal note: 'I tell you, unless you repent, you will all perish as they did.'

It is true, however, that God the Father of Jesus continually keeps an eye on sinners, but he does so in a very different spirit. He does it in the way that is pictured in the parable of the fig tree. The fig tree just stood there, obviously not bearing fruit, something that had been going on already for three years. The owner of the vineyard is now on the verge of losing his patience. 'This fig tree is only wasting the soil here, so it is better to cut it down,' he said to the keeper of the vineyard. But this man still had hope. He was familiar with fig trees and knew that it could take several years before they bore fruit, so he favoured being patient. Wanting to help the process, he said: 'Sir, let it alone for one more year; let me first dig the soil around it and put manure on it. Perhaps it will bear fruit next year.'

Just as the keeper of the vineyard keeps his eye on the fig tree and eagerly looks for the first fruit buds, so God looks at every sinner and at each one of us. He scrupulously keeps an eye out for what could touch our heart, and looks for the secret stirrings of repentance and conversion. To that end he gives us time. God knows that humans are by nature slow and even slothful, and that it takes a long time for us to become mature adults and finally to bear fruit. It has not been given to humans to reach perfection overnight; our conversion requires much time. Nor can we (for no apparent reason) suddenly take the wrong road. Humans are simply that way and God completely understands this, for this is how he made us. For this reason he waits very patiently and gives us time: he lets time do its work.

For that matter we know all too well that we can only make progress with the aid of time, by trial and error, three steps forward and two steps back. We tend to make many resolutions which we quickly forget and which quickly go up in smoke. Every time we begin anew and quietly take our time. We need not be afraid if we misuse the time God the Father has so generously given us in his infinite mercy.

For all the time given us, every day and every hour, are a marvellous gift from God: it is the time of his grace, whose intent is that we should go to him and let ourselves be seized and turned around by his abundant mercy like so many who have gone before us.

God keeps an eye on us sinners, not in order to let us die, but to give us time so that we may repent and find the abundant life. Let us give thanks to the Lord, for he is good, and his love endures forever!

28

Joy in Time of Trial

Certain passages in the gospel are simultaneously awesome and attractive. They are, first of all, awesome because they refer to strange signs, to our desperation and fear, to a universal time of testing which will come over all people like a net (Luke 21:25–36). But they are also extraordinarily attractive, for Jesus describes his 'second coming' thus: seated on a cloud, clothed with power and great glory. His last word is even charged with hope: 'Now when all these things begin to take place, stand up and raise your heads, because your redemption is drawing near.'

'When all these events begin to occur. . . .' Which events? The reference is to the horrors of the time of testing Jesus describes here, a time in which all that is most awesome and most attractive will be mingled together. Suddenly we will be confronted by the horrors of temptation and by Jesus' total absence amidst the time of testing. This is the strange paradox for which the world and the Church are headed and whose extremes can never be separated: the terrors of the testing and the total absence of Jesus.

These two things, in fact, are so inseparably connected one could say the only thing which now still separates us from Jesus is precisely this time of testing. It is not the case that the time of trial, which always only weakens us, would make us inferior in the sight of Jesus. What separates us is the fact that the trial still lies ahead of us, the fact that we have not yet had the opportunity to pass through it to the end. It is the trial that still has to come which keeps us separated from Jesus, a trial which we, as Jesus teaches us, still need to endure, in the dizzying confusion and fear with which every person who looks for this final trial has to cope. Without giving in to despair but in all humility we remain standing, while with a cheerful heart we voice our confidence in prayer and call upon the Name of him whom we expect and love: Lord Jesus, come!

Of this great end-time testing reported by the gospel we daily get a small foretaste in the temptations and disappointments we experience now. Temptations of the flesh or temptations of the spirit, which are even more subtle and dangerous, consistently mirror the same end-time scenario depicted in the gospel account. Keeping in mind the difference in proportion, we can say that they are a foreshadowing of the great end-time trial. Today, as will be the case then, the testing comes upon us unexpectedly and our own resources no longer amount to anything. That time of testing always fascinates us; it also overwhelms us and literally leaves us at our wit's end. That is also how Jesus proleptically describes it; and without all these things it would not be a true temptation, worthy of Jesus and his salvation.

Even though we are unable to remain in control of the temptation, we are nevertheless being asked not to run from it or avoid it. We need to undergo the temptation and to pass through it in order to come to Jesus, and also we need to follow in his footsteps, our eyes focused on his, he in us and we in him. He too, remember, underwent and endured this test. In the bloody agony of Gethsemane he experienced our desperation and dread. He, however, remained awake, for while his apostles slept he surrendered himself in prayer to his Father's love. In every temptation, in the depths of the infatuation of our senses or in the densest darkness

Well done,
good and faithful
servant,
enter
into
the *joy*
of your Lord.

✠

In thanksgiving

for the life

God gave us in our sister

Mary Immaculate of Jesus

Born	31st May 1909
Professed	12th June 1943
Died	5th February 1998

May she rest in Peace

Ware Carmel

of our mind, there is but one way out, for us as well, the way of Jesus: 'Be alert at all times, praying that you may have the strength to escape all these things that will take place and to stand before the Son of Man' (Luke 21:36).

29

A Missed Chance

Just as 'missed chances' occur in the life of every one of
us, so it was in the life of the rich young man in the
gospel (Mark 10:17–30). This young man was not guilty of
anything: from his childhood onwards he had kept all the
commandments. Jesus could not demand anything more
from him. He could in fact have confined himself to con-
gratulating him, had there not been the question of the
young man himself: 'What must I do to inherit eternal
life?' It was a question which went beyond the superficial
complacency he feigned and betrayed a deeper-lying unful-
filled longing.

Indeed, Jesus could not demand anything *more* from him,
but love does not content itself simply with what is strictly
necessary. Mark comments that Jesus' eyes, as they were
focusing on the young man, suddenly began to sparkle.
'Jesus, looking at him, loved him,' he writes. For love always
wants to take the next step; nothing can really satisfy it. So
Jesus, full of love, risked adding: 'There's one thing you still
lack; go, sell what you own and give the money to the poor;
then come, follow me.'

'Follow me': a person can only permanently attach himself
to Jesus out of love. Such a proposal would have sounded
very attractive in the young man's ears had there not been
the condition of divesting himself of all his possessions in
order to follow Jesus as a *poor* person.

The reference here, moreover, is to a non-negotiable condition, for were the young man to question it Jesus would answer that no man can serve two masters at once. Only one who is poor and has shared his possessions with the poor is able to respond to Jesus' offer and follow him. The young man was enormously rich; the tender and probingly loving look of Jesus did not affect him sufficiently. This was really asking too much and, as the evangelist notes, 'he went away grieving'. Although it was his ardent wish to follow Jesus, he decided to pass up this unique opportunity. Jesus grieved as well. He was deeply disappointed in his love and had once again to experience how far wealth separates people from God.

But Jesus did not despair. Although a big opportunity was missed here, it was not the last. For Jesus knows nothing of 'last chances'. For that matter, this is how the lives of human beings and believers with the Lord usually run: a long series of miserably missed chances. But God never gives up hope. What is improbable and even impossible for humans is possible for God: a camel *can* pass through the eye of a needle. This is simply how it usually goes with people: they so often let the first chances pass them by, even the first divine chance, before they allow themselves to be seized by the divinely patient God.

Regardless of who we are and what our spiritual experience is, we always lack something needed to follow Jesus closely. Or perhaps we always possess something superfluous which distances us from his intimate love. Usually we let that which his love seeks laboriously, little by little, to communicate to us slip away from us. When the time comes, however, he will teach us to be detached with an enormous gentleness which only his grace can filter into our heart. No earthly riches of any kind, after all, will permanently stand between Jesus and us, for with sweet insistence his gentleness will conquer the wealth of all people. And those who, like the apostles, have left all their possessions behind for his sake will be given them back a hundredfold. Before they managed to divest themselves of their riches out of love for Jesus, they also clung tightly to them and were, without knowing it, their slaves. The riches which come in their place, however, will be a pure gift from God, a new manifestation of his grace and a source of continual thanksgiving. And the more missed chances occur in our life, the more gloriously God's mercy will manifest itself, and the more irresistibly Jesus' gaze will rest upon the rich young man who is also hidden in each one of us.

30

A Mark of God

When Jesus speaks about the love between a husband and a wife, he does it in a particularly subtle and sensitive way (Mark 10:2–12). He himself, after all, is highly involved in this love – both he and his Father.

When God created humans he created them man and woman, after his image and likeness. Since then an indelible sign of God is present in every human being: it is this tender amazement and this deep desire which irresistibly draws a man and a woman together. At the moment in which they experience the blossoming of love they also, unconsciously, discover an identifying mark of God within themselves. It is like a spark from the enormous fire which is God: Father, Son and Holy Spirit united in a mutual community of love which incessantly drives them towards each other. 'God is love,' says St John, an enormous blaze of love, and the human being who experiences the birth of a small spark of this love in his or her heart immediately begins to sense what God may be like. For St John adds: 'And those who abide in love abide in God, and God abides in them' (1 John 4:16).

To abide in love, to experience love, to link one's life to a love is to take part in God. It is also to take part in Jesus Christ, in that surpassing love, as St Paul put it, which drove him to leave his Father in order to go to the humble sinners who constitute the entire human community, to give his body and blood on the cross and to make his Church into his radiant bride. When St Paul speaks of marriage he consistently compares it to the love-bond between Christ and the Church: 'This is a great mystery, and I am applying it to Christ and the Church' (Eph. 5:32). God at one time conceived the love between a husband and a wife in this fashion, says the gospel, but that was 'in the beginning, at the creation'.

However, there exists a large gap between the image and the reality, between this mark of God in us and what we have made of it. God, however, refuses to be discouraged; he is patient with us. His image in us is so grand, his mark so demanding, that many centuries of step-by-step guidelines of God were needed before humans had an inkling of it and could begin to live with it.

On account of 'the hardness of our heart' God for a long time tolerated divorce. Some semblance of his image continued to exist but in a reduced and unfinished state, powerless to come to full maturity. In Jesus' day marriages were contracted and dissolved and the scribes questioned the practice; even the apostles had not yet completely settled the question: 'Is a man free to send away his wife?' But the original divine plan remained unchanged: 'What God has joined together, let no human break up.' Only this divine plan can let something shine through in the love between a man and his wife of the blaze of love which is God himself.

Even in our society today, where marriages are still being contracted and dissolved, the original plan of God will remain intact. All the stirrings of love, even the most minimal attraction of love, teach us something very important about God. It is a divine mark within us by which we can again turn to him and know that he is there, that we came forth from his hands and that we belong to him forever.

God's love is so great that the most minute manifestation of it again unbreakably links all humans to him.

But also today we still remain far removed from the full unfolding of that love within us. Frequently that image is very murky and uncertain, almost unrecognisable even, because love remains restricted to a small circle: it cannot sprout wings and expand and from the start remains imprisoned within a chrysalis of inevitable narcissism. Often, therefore, love ends with the breaking of the commitment that was made and thus injures the image God has deposited in each one of us. Who will be surprised at this? How could we appeal to that love if Jesus had not come? Some day his love-unto-death, to which we on our part also completely dare to surrender ourselves, will heal us.

31

Only Love Is Not Blind

The closer one comes to Jesus, the harder it is to recognise him. This was especially true for his contemporaries, even though we are perhaps inclined to believe the opposite (Mark 6:1–6). They had all grown up with Jesus, knew his parents and were familiar with both his good and his bad sides. Yet the better they knew Jesus the higher was the wall that kept them from recognising him. This, however, did not surprise Jesus: 'Prophets are not without honour, except in their hometown, and among their own kin, and in their own house' (Mark 6:4).

Must this indeed be so? Must Jesus' humanity always erect a screen between us and his divinity? Must Jesus' human body obscure the glory of his divine Sonship? Certainly not: the New Testament clearly indicates that Jesus' humanity bore the exact imprint of the divine, the 'reflection of the glory of God' (Heb. 1:3). Three apostles were present on Mount Tabor when Jesus appeared to them bodily, radiant with divine light, and his divinity was lit up so brilliantly they became fearful and completely confused. No, in Jesus God became human so that all might recognise and see God through him. He could hardly have put it more clearly: 'Those who have seen me have seen the Father.'

Then how is it that some – and usually those who were very close to him – remained blind to Jesus' identity? And how come others – strangers or pagans – recognised him without hesitation? This question continues to occupy us today because the Church asserts that Jesus has risen from the dead but we still have the greatest difficulty recognising him as a God who lives among us.

Jesus himself 'was amazed at their unbelief'. The distinction between those who see and those who do not see is rooted in faith or its absence. The light which breaks through the veil of Jesus' body and makes it transparent to the glory of God is our faith: 'Believe and you will see the glory of God', he was to say to Mary at the grave of her brother Lazarus.

As long as we have not yet received the gift of faith in its fullness, the problem is not the proximity of Jesus in time or space, or the question of whether we belong to his closest relatives, or lack of knowledge or skill; the problem is the wall, our blindness, which still remains and will inevitably become worse.

There is nothing we can do about that. Neither any exertion of our own, nor our good will can furnish us the gift of faith: 'No one can come to me unless drawn by the Father who sent me,' says Jesus (John 6:44). We can only recognise him if this mysterious drawing power comes into effect, if the Father chooses us so that his Son can be recognised by us.

And this drawing power is a matter of love; this choice is an election of love. The veil which covers Jesus' face can only be lifted or removed by love.

That so many people do not or can no longer recognise Jesus need not surprise us any more than the doubts which often besiege us and which seem to threaten our faith. For only the Holy Spirit can utter the faith we received in baptism; only he can pray in us as we ought to pray. It is enough for us to let ourselves be seized by the prayer of the

Holy Spirit in the depths of our heart. That is the cry of faith which arises from us: 'Lord Jesus, to whom can we go? You have the words of eternal life.' 'Lord Jesus, I believe; help my unbelief' (John 6:68; Mark 9:24).

32

The Mysteries of the Kingdom

'The wise and the intelligent': these are two qualifications which people today greatly appreciate. Wisdom is a virtue and knowledge a skill which people rightly pursue. Jesus does not in any way reject these things. He simply observes that his father has not designated the wise and intelligent as those to whom he reveals the mysteries of the Kingdom. Not only has he not revealed these mysteries to them but he actively conceals them so that they will have no knowledge of them (Matt. 11:25–30).

Why are the wise and intelligent thus rejected? Jesus does not tell us openly. Nevertheless he stresses that the decision is completely dependent on the free will of the Father: 'Yes, Father, for such was your gracious will' (Matt. 11:26). If there is a preference it is because the Father so wills it. At play here is not chance, nor a form of coercion, but a free choice which to our minds carries with it a suggestion of arbitrariness.

This is no more than appearance, however, for the Father takes no pleasure in rejecting people and hiding things. If he conceals something from some people his main concern is still to create joy in the hearts of the recipients of revelation. The Father has priorities which differ from ours and they are amazing. And if a tinge of arbitrariness comes through, it is the arbitrariness of love. The first movement of his love is aimed, not at the wise and intelligent, at those who have insight and knowledge, but at 'infants', says Jesus.

Who are these 'infants'? St Paul, in one of his letters, touches on the same theme – the Father's preference for the smallest of the lot – and offers a description. He is referring to those who are of no account in the eyes of the world, people of no value, 'nothing-people', or those who simply do not exist in the eyes of others. Is he speaking of cultural and material poverty? Perhaps. Of spiritual poverty? Certainly. God, says St Paul, chose these 'worthless' people so that no flesh might boast in his presence. God chose them because they knew nothing and knew they knew nothing; he chose them because they are capable of nothing and therefore could not resist God, defenceless as they were before his choice and grace.

We must indeed be small not to oppose the revelation God wants to grant us, a revelation so astonishing that it could only make us rigid in our refusal – we who presume to know, who believe we are wise and intelligent. The revelation comes from the Father and the Son and from the special love-bond which so intimately unites them in the Spirit. But how could we ever find God except by putting ourselves more or less in the place of the Son? And how can we know the Son unless we first know the Father? Jesus therefore solemnly declares: 'No one knows the Father except the Son and anyone to whom the Son chooses to reveal him' (Matt. 11:27).

In the Kingdom of Jesus, to stand on the side of the wise or on that of little ones is a choice which continually presents itself to us and will always remain extremely delicate. To choose the side of the poor and to be their advocate is fairly easy, easier in many cases than it will be some day to join their side before the face of God as poor as or even poorer than they are. For what is required of us – or offered to us – is a very different nature, one that surpasses all knowledge and all charity. It concerns the only thing that is absolutely necessary, of which we can only say that we have not yet received it, but for which we long with a passion and pray every day. For only Jesus can teach it to us by his association with us: 'Learn from me; for I am gentle and humble in heart, and you will find rest for your souls' (Matt. 11:29). And through this rest and this peace of your heart many around you will be saved.

33

The Cross Not Chosen

The day will come when Jesus will stand between his disciples and their closest relatives: father, mother, son, daughter. These words of the gospel are just as formidable as the summons that Jesus addresses to us when he says, 'whoever does not take up the cross and follow me is not worthy of me' (Matt. 10:37–42).

At first we may hope that these rather harsh words of Jesus, when seen alongside countless others which are much more comforting, are not intended for us and that we may perhaps escape them. We may also believe that they are intended only for a small part of Jesus' flock: for those who have opted for a life of detachment. But if we listen closely to his words, we note that nothing in them gives us licence to take them in that restricted sense.

Jesus indeed recommends life-choices which are optional for Christians, as, for example, abstaining from marriage or selling all one's goods. Not all people are placed under such claims, says Jesus, because the call to such a life is not issued to all – and this is aside from any question of guilt. The pathways can be very unlike each other but there is one main road, one that is not optional. For every disciple of Jesus the journey will always be a cross-bearing journey. The cross is never a matter of choice; it is an integral part of the journey. There is no other choice than the cross that is offered to us all. We have no choice but to accept it. But that is enough.

That might seem easy enough but we all know that a cross is not always equally pleasant. If the words of Jesus concerning the cross often hit us hard, the Holy Spirit of Jesus in our everyday life fortunately operates very differently – with infinite tenderness and care. He takes many years over the job, obviously giving us a time of 'carefreeness' and success to prepare us in peace for our own cross, for the decision which in an instant can turn our entire life in the direction of previously unsuspected depths of faith and love.

I say 'in an instant', for when our hour has really arrived, God's grace will also be there, and very small things may suffice to help in our simple acceptance of and co-operation with grace. What counts is the recognition of our real cross. Often it is much more difficult to recognise the cross Jesus intends for us personally than to accept it once we have recognised it. We are inclined to think, furthermore, that our crosses would not be so painful if we could immediately see them. There lies the rub which usually disturbs those who have opted for a life of detachment. Their temptation consists in imagining that they already know beforehand what their cross or time of testing will be. Unfortunately, a cross one knows in advance, even if it is fairly heavy, is no longer the cross of Jesus. Our real cross is always to some degree unanticipated and always seems to far surpass our strength. As a rule, we would never have chosen it. Passionately to cling to a cross of our own choosing and perhaps unconsciously but equally passionately to reject the cross that Jesus intends for us is perhaps the heaviest and most discouraging cross. It could keep us forever from taking up our real cross if Jesus did not at some time intervene.

For what is our cross other than Jesus himself? To accept this cross is to accept him. It is simultaneously 'to take up our cross' and to follow him. Undoubtedly, if we could know God's gift, if we could see and recognise it, we would not have an easier time of it.

34

The Deepest Kind of Thirst

Jesus and the Samaritan woman met each other at the well of Sychar. He was thirsty, so was she; both waited for the water that would be drawn up from the well (John 4:5–42).

But the two of them experienced this banal waiting period differently. For Jesus it had a set of implications it didn't yet have for the woman. Jesus, of course, saw things much more deeply. He discerned their hidden meaning. To him every visible reality evokes another that is still provisionally outside our range of vision. Everything speaks a language to him; everything is a sign and a sacrament; all things sing of the glory and love of his Father: this water, this well, the thirst which both of them feel, this desire to drink, even the unbearable thirst of the Samaritan woman. It was a thirst she carried with her everywhere from man to man without being able to quench it, until she no longer knew who her true husband and what true love was.

Jesus' thirst was the result of a long trek over hot, dusty roads. 'Give me a drink,' he said to the woman. But he immediately linked his own thirst to another kind of thirst. Jesus had a deeper thirst for this Samaritan woman than for water, for this woman who as yet did not know of his real thirst, that other thirst with all its torment. Jesus thirsted for a chance to quench that other thirst, to give this woman – who as yet did not know how Jesus himself was going to address her – to drink: 'If you knew the gift of God, and who it is that is saying to you, "Give me a drink," you would have asked him, and he would have given you living water.'

The Samaritan woman, too, was thirsty, a thirst that was much deeper than she herself knew. Jesus' presence held her spellbound and his words confused her. Contrary to all customs, he not only presumed to ask her for some water, but against all expectation he offered her a mysterious kind of water, *living* water that quenches every thirst forever and becomes for everyone who drinks it a wellspring of eternal life. Such an offer, even though the woman did not immediately grasp its meaning, was irresistible: 'Sir, give me this water so that I may never be thirsty again!'

To Jesus everything was clear – this well, this water, this terrible thirst, her succession of five husbands, this poor woman's fruitless floundering in love. Everything pointed to the same mystery: that other spring which Jesus always wants to open up in the heart of every person, so that it may always flow and satisfy and finally gush up to the eternal life of the Father in love and thanksgiving.

For the Father also yearns and thirsts. Jesus made this more specific for the benefit of the Samaritan woman in the following words: 'the Father seeks those who will worship him in spirit and truth'. Henceforth people will no longer worship the Father at the usual places of prayer – Mount Gerizim for the Samaritans or the temple in Jerusalem for orthodox Jews. It will only occur where the spring of living water gushes up, of which we can drink without ever becoming thirsty again, where from now on Jesus becomes our temple – in the depths of our heart.

Located in the depths of our heart, where Jesus touched the Samaritan woman, is the centre of all thirst and yearning. There, first of all, our own thirst originates, the thirst which in all sorts of ways continually torments us but which can never be quenched by any earthly drink, because all our yearnings, even the most unusual ones, are merely very temporary manifestations of an infinitely deeper hidden yearning. Next, we also find there the thirst of Jesus, who intensely wants to give us to drink from the living water which he alone knows and can cause to bubble up in our heart. Finally, there is the thirst of the Father, who is continually in search of people who will worship him in spirit and truth. All these languishing, longing forms of thirst are the thirst of the entire universe which exists in our heart and begs to be quenched: 'Lord Jesus, give me some of that water as well, that I may never be thirsty again.'

35

Omnipotence in Poverty

Since Jesus came to live among us, God's omnipotence has erupted over the world. First, for a long period, it remained obscure and seemed hidden. It was there nevertheless and capable in the blink of an eye of changing the outlook of the world. Over time it gradually surfaced, first on a very modest scale, sometimes as if it sought to break forth from his healing body, and in that connection Jesus insisted on the strictest silence. But in vain: rumour ever more swiftly made the rounds, spreading like wildfire in cities and villages. Everybody was talking about it: a prophet has arisen among us. Many people had seen that the demon-possessed and the sick were healed, the dead raised, and even a potentially dangerous storm had been stilled.

Now for the first time Jesus began to share this omnipotence with his disciples. The gospel expressly tells us: 'he gave them authority over unclean spirits'. 'They cast out many demons, and anointed with oil many who were sick and cured them' (Mark 6:7–13). Jesus came to bring fire on earth and how intensely he wished it were already kindled (Luke 12:49). He brought God's omnipotence into the world and wished above all that it would spread and become effective: that it would bring healing, power and encouragement, that it would generate life everywhere.

Even though the time of Jesus is long past, that power of his is still always present; more than ever before it is in our midst and able to inject a new dynamic into the world. In this regard Jesus' return to his Father made no difference whatever. On the contrary, at the very moment Jesus was about to ascend to heaven, he once more solemnly gave his assurance that his presence and activity would remain in the midst of his Church. Signs and wonders would everywhere accompany those who believed in his word to the end of time.

This divine omnipotence of Jesus is still present and available to his Church and to us. As in the days of Jesus, it sometimes remains very modest; it is not always visible to the naked eye and seems to conceal itself. The stronger it is, the less tangible and measurable it seems. It falls outside of our statistics and all our learned research. Jesus seems, for that matter, to have foreseen all this. To his mind the extraordinary power the apostles received brought with it an equally extraordinary poverty: they must not take anything with them except a staff, not even bread or money; they must be content with a pair of sandals and one garment; they would consistently be at the mercy of the good will or ill will of those who received them. The greater and more irresistible the divine power that was given to the apostles, the more uncertain and dubious would be the human means at their disposal.

And this applied not just to the degree of comfort and convenience with which they would exercise their apostle-ship but also to the word they would proclaim. If they were dragged before the synagogues, or had to stand face-to-face before the great officials of the earth, it would be pointless for them to prepare a carefully composed testimony: instead, words would be put in their mouths, for the Holy Spirit would witness through them.

God, as the Lord and architect of his Kingdom, chooses the means. The disciples, whoever they are, can only offer him the means they have received from him. How utterly disproportionate is the ratio between human power and the omnipotence of God, between human words and the word of the Lord. In the depths of this inadequacy the disciple can only let himself or herself be seized by the grace of God, who will transform the human means by his own power, a grace that will always remain the same in a Church that is humble and poor, a Church which will over and over again repeat his miracles.

36

Being Patient with Weeds

Jesus' disciples were impatient. The weeds which began to shoot up amid the wheat disturbed, even irritated, them. There was no time to lose, they thought, and stood ready to go at them (Matt. 13:25ff.).

Why did Jesus' disciples get so excited at the sight of all those weeds? They were probably not able to conduct a deep analysis of their reactions, though certainly in their eyes countless good reasons could be cited for going after the weeds. Where did the weeds come from? What do they mean and what danger do they present? What risks do the disciples run if they delay? The disciples do not entertain these and other rational considerations. Certainly, tracing the causes argues in favour of the disciples' competence and sense of duty, but neither the inspiration nor the urge for eradicating the spreading weeds is explained: 'Lord, do you want us to go and gather them?'

If the weeds annoyed the disciples that much, it was presumably because this matter was of personal concern to them, more than they were able to admit. The weeds touched something deep within them, a very sad spot they would rather banish from their heart, eradicate even, destroy once and for all, and never speak of again. The sight of these weeds opened up in them a wound which was not completely healed, whose scars they wanted to stash away at any cost and whose memory had been subtly suppressed. And it is certainly true that the sight of weeds in the

Kingdom of Jesus, whether in the Church or in the heart of our brothers, will always cause us pain. It prompts the thought that the good seed is also threatened by the weeds in our heart – a sad reminder which goads us strongly into wanting to take up arms against all the evil of the whole world, against all the evil that exists in the lives of others, rather than being willing to look at the weeds which thrive so vigorously in our own heart.

Things are very different with Jesus; he never gets excited when he surveys the weeds; they leave him unmoved. Why? He, of course, also recognises these weeds and knows all too well where they come from. The one who sowed them is the enemy. How could it be otherwise for him who awaits the harvest? This is how it goes for the Church and all its children on an earth where the prince of this world has not yet been expelled for good. However, it is pointless for us immediately – in our own strength and with our own means – to pull up the weeds, for several reasons. In the first place, Jesus knows that he can trust the good seed. His vitality is irresistible and the humble patience of the sower will culmi-nate in the conquest of evil. But Jesus especially reminds the disciples that, in destroying the weeds, they will at the same time run the risk of damaging the good grain. For it is not enough to hurl ourselves, like hardhearted judges, upon the evil existing in others. We must genuinely be able to tell the weeds from the grain, to discriminate between the really good and the really evil.

Yet evil as such is never so deceptive that it can succeed in passing itself off as good and in representing good as evil. Be careful, Jesus would say, that you are not deluded by the disguise which one so often encounters here on earth before the hour of the harvest dawns, a disguise no one less than the arch-enemy has put together. Indeed, what sort of perfection or thirst for righteousness gives us the right to destroy the imperfect and unrighteous? And where do we find a person who is so thoroughly evil that he or she deserves forever to be excluded from every form of mercy? How can we accurately measure the straw in the eye of a brother if we are afraid of looking at the beam in our own eye? Until Jesus' return only one attitude is possible, the one displayed by the Lord of the harvest himself: exercise patience towards evil, both the evil of others and your own, for this infinite patience and humble tolerance are to God like the eyes of his mercy.

37

Fuel for the Fire of Love

Luke's account of the call of the disciple Peter shows the enormous importance of this event (Luke 5:1–11). Not primarily because the hour has struck in which Peter is called to follow Jesus and leave everything behind, but especially because of what precedes the event.

Jesus, it seems, was not a complete stranger to Peter. When the crowd which came to listen to him on the lake-shore was pressing in on him, Jesus took the liberty of inviting himself to come aboard Peter's fishing boat in order to speak to the crowd more easily. Peter, on his part, probably felt a certain respect for this brilliant youthful rabbi, perhaps even a feeling of friendship. After Jesus had ended his speech he asked Peter to put out into deeper water and go fishing.

That was when the miracle happened. Peter, seeing it, was astonished. At that moment he recognised Jesus: '*Kurios*, Lord,' he called him and fell on his knees. But what was it that made him recognise Jesus? The miraculous catch of fish had certainly been sensational but was no more than an external sign. It did not compare with the other miracle which occurred in Peter's heart and which had disturbed him even more. Suddenly he felt he was a sinner: 'Lord, go away from me, for I am a sinful man!'

Peter knew, of course, that he was no saint. He was certainly aware of his failings. He had his good side and his bad side, like everyone else; he was neither better nor worse than the others. But from this point on things were going to be different. The one confronting him is no longer an ordinary rabbi but the Saviour of the world, he who came not for the righteous but for sinners. By recognising Jesus, Peter had become acutely conscious of his own sinfulness. The situation was not that he first discovered his sins and then Jesus, nor the reverse; the whole thing happened all at once and, amazingly enough, because he now knew himself to be a sinner.

Every believer is called to the same experience. What do we know about Jesus before we have understood him? A name? An image? A formula from a catechism? Extremely little. The most comprehensive theological theories, the most fascinating exegetical discoveries can only start us on our way, but none of these things can make us really feel Jesus' presence.

And what do we know about sin, our sins, before we have thus met Jesus? A series of commandments which have fascinated one group of people and paralysed another? A vague sense of guilt which pursues us day and night to sour even our smallest pleasures? Or worse, a feeling of having once and for all succeeded in becoming free from sin and being on the side of the irreproachable and righteous?

Only Jesus can reveal to us our true sinfulness and so make it bearable. Bearable because even our sin is fuel for the fire of love, because at the moment when our sin is revealed it is already forgiven. Only the consciousness that our sin has been forgiven, a 'sweet and joyful repentance' as our fathers called it, can give us the assurance that we have really met Jesus, not the Jesus of learned scholars and theologians, but the Jesus who loved me when I was still a sinner and gave himself up for me.

And the better I know him, the more I will remember to love him – and the more sinful I will feel, but as a sinner who has been granted forgiveness, in ongoing gratitude forever. There is no other miracle and no other way: 'One to whom little is forgiven, loves little' said Jesus (Luke 7:47). One to whom much has been forgiven is capable of much love.

38

Which God Is Dead?

The error of the unprofitable servant was not so much his negligence and sloth, but the fact that he was mistaken about God: 'Master, I knew that you were a harsh man, reaping where you did not sow and gathering where you did not scatter seed, so I was afraid, and I went and hid your talent in the ground' (Matt. 25:14–30). This God, a severe master, implacably demanding down to the smallest things, is not the Father Jesus knew and recognised from his experience. Unfortunately, he added, those who settle for a God who is a human invention will one day be treated, without mercy, in terms of the image they themselves have designed: 'So take the talent from him, and give it to the one with the ten talents.'

Every one of us has fashioned an image of God that to some extent is true but at the same time falls far short of the truth. It is probably even more false than true. The more we affirm something about God, as St Thomas Aquinas has already pointed out, the more we are in error; and the more we deny something about him, the closer we are to the truth. We speak the truth about God only when we affirm what he is not.

Certain theologians were so struck by the distance between what we say about God and what we suspect is true about him that they proceeded to proclaim a theology of the death of God. This occurred about thirty years ago and at the time caused a lot of commotion, perhaps altogether mistakenly. For what they really meant to say was that for a true encounter with God all the concepts of theology are inadequate. The image of God we had constructed for ourselves was dead or bound to die, for God was altogether different, and so in part these theologians were right.

Nevertheless we are still always talking about God. We tend to propagate a certain *a priori* image of God which guides us. It is perhaps an image we remember from the catechism or one inherited from our parents. Perhaps we think we have found it ourselves in personal reading or study. This image lies deeply hidden within us in the place where all earlier memories have accumulated, memories we have probably forgotten but which, despite ourselves, still exert a secret influence. These are the many traces of the love aroused within us, a love that was received, refused or perhaps rejected by us; now they are merely an inextricable tangle of longings, hurts and frustrations. At a still deeper level, quite apart from our conscious will, our God-image is part of a dark, collective inheritance not one of us can escape. This is true to the degree that anyone who today says that God is dead only confirms, in an extremely indirect way, that he exists.

The image of God is like something innate, an image that continually needs to be evangelised, so that we do not repeat the mistake made by the unprofitable servant who was wrong about God. And this familiar image of God, implanted in us by nature, is something like a summons, something that cannot exist by itself. It must not only be purified but actually executed in order to arise anew in an experience of faith. Only those who, on a certain day, from within a sort of profound amazement, have really encountered God will be able to surmise somewhat what he is really like. The words of God in Scripture and especially in the gospel are the most common place for the origination of such amaze-ment. But on our life's journey there are other possibilities as well: a mother's heart or a father's strength, the pure smile of a child, the eyes of two lovers finding peace in each other, the extended hand of a poor person, the desperation of a sick person, but especially our own failures, times in which God, in profound compassion, extended to us his helping hand. Wherever God encounters us in Jesus Christ, our most assured ideas about him seem to be shattered and we are, as it were, blinded by the first rays of his glory. For God is always greater than our heart.

39

Alone with His Father

'If you are looking for me, then let these men go,' said Jesus (John 18:8). And he in fact went out to meet the mystery of death alone and in profound solitude. From the time they were in the Garden of Gethsemane Jesus made certain that his disciples would not be mistaken for him and could make their escape. Yet some of them wanted to follow him as far as they possibly could. 'Let us also go, that we may die with him,' Thomas had said a few days earlier when Jesus was on the point of going to Lazarus' tomb (John 11:16). And Peter especially had sworn that he would stay with him to the point of dying with him, an assertion Jesus had then firmly rejected by saying: 'Where I am going you cannot follow me now but you will later' (John 13:36). In this hour, after all, Jesus had to face death completely alone.

In the course of his suffering this loneliness became ever more intense and more anxious. The disciples fled at sight of the soldiers; only Jesus' two most faithful friends, Peter and John, were to return, timidly and from a safe distance following their Master as far as the courtyard of the high priest. Thus, unfortunately, Peter ran into the trap set for him by a maid. He then denied and abandoned Jesus. Instead of following Jesus, he shamefully retreated.

Before the judgement seat of Pilate all the people left Jesus in the lurch. These same people, walking through the same streets only a few days before, had welcomed him in triumph as the Messiah: 'Hosanna, Son of David!' was their cry. But Jesus was not surprised at being deserted by the Jews. He even justified this desertion before Pilate who interrogated him about the kingship he claimed for himself and about his Kingdom. His Kingdom was not of this world, a world in which Jesus must have felt alone and like a stranger. If his Kingdom had been of this world, he declared before Pilate, his followers would have fought for him and he would not have been delivered up to the Jews.

Only John, the beloved disciple, along with the mother of Jesus and a few more women, had succeeded in reaching Golgotha. There they stood beneath the cross, the terminal point of their humble but unremitting love. And there Jesus himself could take the initiative in releasing himself from the last ties of friendship which still bound his heart to this earth. He entrusted his mother Mary to John and John to his mother, and so everything was fulfilled. Had Jesus now divested himself of everything and did he now stand naked before the yawning darkness of death – totally alone? Not so. He stood before his Father and his death was no longer a death but a transition into the hands of his Father: 'Father into your hands I commend my spirit.'

Just a few days before, when Jesus had seen this hour of abandonment and intense loneliness coming, he had explained its meaning. 'The hour is coming, indeed it has come, when you will be scattered, each one to his own home, and you will leave me alone. Yet I am not alone because the Father is with me' (John 16:32). Even in the solitariness of his death Jesus was not alone. His earthly existence could end only in the arms of his heavenly Father.

'Where I am going, you cannot follow me now but you will later.' For the disciples of Jesus the loneliness of death was only temporary as it is also for us. Nevertheless we have all been forewarned for the day that our hour comes. Our loneliness will become ever clearer as time passes; one after another, all our resources and weapons will drop away, and all our connections will snap. It will no longer be our work; it will be Jesus who will make it his concern. But we have nothing to fear, for from now on the passage is free. Jesus himself opened it for us and he himself, as the first to do so, passed through it on his cross. Just as he was never alone, so we too will never be alone, for even in the shadow of death Jesus will always be with us.

40

Apart from Jesus

From our baptism we have all been branches of the one true vine. From that moment on Jesus' life became the secret source of our life, a spring of life which incessantly and very quietly keeps bubbling up in the depths of our heart. All we do and say, all our prayers and everything we are, is given us freely from this source.

This can only continue, however, on one condition, a condition to which Jesus continually returns in the gospel: the branches must remain in the vine; that is, we must remain in Jesus, mysteriously connected with this divine source of life, which we carry deep in our heart everywhere (John 15:1–8). It is indeed always there; it is always at our disposal, whereas we ourselves are not always available. Our thoughts may be elsewhere, we may even distance ourselves from that source, we may walk, talk and pray having already broken our contact with the life-force and vitality of the vine, with the life of Jesus that lives in us. It is even quite easy to do this; in fact numerous believers often live in detachment from their deepest source of life without noticing it themselves. This does not always happen intentionally but frequently simply as a result of inattention. After all, how many people fix their attention on the riches of this divine lifeline, this spring of life which keeps bubbling up in their heart? Hence they are not at all guilty of anything, they are only ignorant or inexperienced; they do not know that Jesus is the only source for them and have no idea of the consequences for their life.

The result, accordingly, is not surprising: many people are like the branches that have been pulled from the vine and die, says Jesus. They are gathered up and thrown into the fire. Or to use another image from this section of the gospel: they are for the time being unfruitful; they do not yet bear fruit, certainly not the fruit which the Father expects from them and which they cannot bear as long as the branch remains separate from the vine that is Jesus. 'Just as the branch cannot bear fruit by itself unless it abides in the vine, neither can you unless you abide in me . . . for apart from me you can do nothing.'

True, we can pretend we are doing something and utter words we ourselves have dreamed up or start the umpteenth project of our own invention. We can improvise an unprecedented prayer and think we are very original. But the words will never be those which Jesus would have put on our lips, nor will the deeds be those which Jesus would have wanted to inspire in us, nor will it be the prayer that he had already begun to pray deep within us. We do not hear him, simply because we have not remained in him, separated as we are from Jesus, our vine. We do from time to time ask for an explanation for what Jesus calls 'withering'. And many others notice this as well. For despite all the clever manoeuvres and the nervous gestures which proceed from our good intentions, we come across as very unconvincing. The grapes growing on our branches are green and often very tart.

Still it is enough to continue believing in Jesus, like the branch which remains in the vine, to bear abundant fruit, fruit the Father himself intended for us that they might reveal his glory: 'My Father is glorified by this that you bear much fruit.' Spontaneous fruitbearing, without effort, as the product of a spring which is the life of Jesus, is lodged deeply within us. What exertions would the branch itself have to make to let grapes grow and ripen to maturity? It is enough simply to let the sap rise up for as long as it remains united to the vine. So we, too, must remain united with Jesus in the depths of our heart: 'Those who abide in me and I in them bear much fruit. . . .'

41

Touched by the Father

When manna fell down from heaven in the wilderness, the Israelites complained: they were deeply discouraged and disgusted. And when Jesus, who was the new bread, come down from heaven, the Jews again complained: they did not understand him and refused to recognise him (John 6:41–51).

This was not what might have been expected. If Jesus was truly the new bread which the Father gave to the world that the world might live through him, then was it really so difficult to find out who he was? And should not the famished crowd have thrust itself upon him to satisfy its hunger on him? But no: far from pressing themselves upon him, the Jews severely and vehemently criticised him. This man, whose father and mother as well as other relatives were known to them, could not possibly have come down from heaven.

This did not astonish or offend Jesus. He did not, therefore, reproach his unbelieving listeners. The fact that they did not recognise him seemed quite normal to him. Nothing was less self-evident than Jesus' identity. For no one could claim to know Jesus on the strength of his own resources: 'No one can come to me unless drawn by the Father who sent me.' The hour announced by the prophets, the hour in which 'all would be taught by God' – and that without intermediaries – had now dawned.

Now neither the Law nor the prophets, nor the priests,

the temple or the sacrifices, had lapsed, yet everything would be totally different in the future. For from now on, behind the ancient institution with its signs and rites and much more, there was the secret drawing power of the Father in the depths of human hearts, a force of attraction which would gradually disclose the new meaning of the Law, the new meaning which was Jesus himself. From this time on it would be sufficient for people to believe in Jesus, who was far above the Law and the institutions, and to follow him at his Word: 'Those who believe in me have eternal life', the life that is nurtured by this new bread. If today we can still jointly celebrate the Eucharist, this happens because we too cannot remain insensitive to that mysterious drawing power exerted by the Father. It strikes us in a word from Scripture, by the presence of a brother, by the smile on the face of a sister, by the intoxication which sometimes comes to us from a beautiful liturgy, or in the deep silence of our own heart where we are totally alone with that attraction. And the Father who from now on touches us by his drawing power from within will never again let us go. Just as the prophets have proclaimed, we too have become his pupils, and he continually proceeds to touch us with his infinite gentleness.

Even the word 'gentleness' is saying too much. For no human word is even remotely adequate to convey correctly this mysterious touch of the Father. Any description is either too strong or too weak but in the most basic modesty it is real in the strongest sense of the word: it is pregnant with a reality which surpasses everything else, the only reality worth yearning for with love and patience, the only reality to which we can without qualification, surrender ourselves in all humility and simplicity.

'Unless drawn by the Father . . .' It is impossible for us to recognise Jesus or to hear his voice, still less to follow or proclaim him, unless the Father draws us to him. All our solemn declarations and protests, all the word-mongering in which we indulge with such pleasure, means very little by comparison with the drawing power which issues from the Father in the depths of our heart. All the commotion we create often takes far too much time and is usually accompanied by far too much noise, so that we can hardly sufficiently take note of that drawing power itself. All those false sounds on the surface of things only weaken our inner sensitivity which prompts us all individually to discover that the hour in which we can be taught by God himself has dawned. Then all other things lose their acute urgency; then we do well to remain very quiet, open to the touch of the Father which will undoubtedly take us on to the right road.

42

Surprised by Compassion

At the sight of the crowd which had gathered on the shore of the lake in order to see him, Jesus was seized by compassion, says the evangelist, for they were like sheep without a shepherd (Mark 6:30–34).

Deep within him Jesus was moved to compassion. For this he had left his Father and come among us to share our human existence. This was the only reason for the movement of mercy which started in Mary's womb and culminated on the cross and in the resurrection. That was the only motive – completely irrational – for what to God was an ordinary process: love, a heartfelt love, tender and deeply affected by the sight of our misery. Jesus' entire life right up to his death was the most concrete sign, the most tangible proof, of this love. As St Paul put it: 'He loved me and gave himself for me' (Gal. 2:20).

The two events which follow in this section of the gospel are a clear illustration of it. First there is Jesus' love for his disciples, love which is extremely sensitive. They had come back from their first mission tour and reported on the first successes they had achieved and the first miracles they had performed. They were proud but exhausted. The people had come in large numbers. On account of their many activities they had barely had time to eat. Jesus now invited them to follow him to a quiet deserted spot which he alone knew and where they could take a break with him.

To escape the pressures of action, to rest in the company

of Jesus, to take time for him and for ourselves, to enjoy the luxury of intimacy together – all this is sometimes as important and necessary as the brilliance of a successful mission. Jesus was with the disciples in the glow of the action as they tasted the joy of proclaiming his name; he was with them as well when he took them along for a time of intimacy. The disciples, for that matter, had no time to choose. In both cases Jesus was in charge. It is he who chooses us and who, every day anew, knows what is good for us. It is most important to let him choose, to let ourselves be chosen by him.

On the other side of the lake a surprise awaited the disciples, and Jesus too. The people had guessed what Jesus was up to and so they had gone ahead to the lakeshore and waited for him there. Again it was love and mercy which settled things for Jesus. At the sight of the crowd he did not hesitate for a moment. These people were bent on meeting the Master who would teach them, a shepherd who would lead them. And to that end, of course, he had come. Again his heart was filled with joy, for Jesus was never more himself than when he could show mercy and compassion.

Today, some twenty centuries later, this is still true for every one of us. We too are like sheep in search of a shepherd, disciples hungry for the word of a master teacher. For this reason he came to us and follows at our heels from the moment of our birth, even through all the detours, twists and coils of our confused life-pattern. And the more we have been injured by life, the farther we have strayed, the more his heart which always follows us will be concerned about us, even without our knowing it. It is not his purpose to spy on us and perhaps to catch us in doing something wrong, or to rain down accusations upon us, or to condemn us. Always he will invite us to come and rest with him at the other side of the lake: 'Come to me, all you who are exhausted and heavy laden and I will give you rest and relief!' (Matt. 11:28).

43

Love Which Makes Itself Small

'Now before the festival of the Passover, Jesus knew that his hour had come. . . .' This, finally, is the decisive hour in which Jesus enters his passion and resurrection. The account sounds solemn and moving. Now, with his disciples around him, Jesus wanted to share with them, in the form of a testament or memento, the most precious thing he possessed (John 13:1–15). For that reason Jesus wanted to perform significant and symbolic actions which could be readily understood, signs which would prefigure the mystery that was about to happen and which would forever be a most precious memory to his disciples when he himself was no longer there. Matthew, Mark and Luke on the one hand, and John on the other, did not, in their respective gospel narratives, record the same signs. The former write of the signs of bread and wine, while John seems to be particularly caught up in the spell of the Servant who kneels at the feet of his disciples. These are two different, but complementary, signs of the self-same mystery.

No one can suspect John of paying too little attention to the Eucharist, because he has recorded, with an amazing realism of flesh and blood, the impressive discourses concerning the bread of life. But for him, at the decisive hour of Easter, the delivered-up flesh and shed blood had to yield to the humble Servant who kneeled down before his brothers before taking his definitive leave from them. Why was that? Did this sign perhaps seem to him more moving and more deeply significant? Does it represent John's personal preference? Who can tell?

In Jesus' eyes these two signs are equally important; they were both intended to be repeated after his death and both are fundamental to the priesthood. There is the priesthood of bread and wine: 'Do this in remembrance of me.' And there is the priesthood of the Servant, to be carried out in loving humility: 'I have set you an example, that you also should do as I have done to you.' These are not two different things but aspects of one and the same priesthood, in connection with which a disciple can never stand above his Master.

Initially the apostles did not understand the two signs, and Peter in particular openly registered resistance. Peter had opened his mouth in protest when Jesus announced his death and now Peter is at the point of forbidding Jesus to wash his feet. Both the sign of the delivered-up body and the sign of humble love seem equally alien to his understanding of what a Messiah in Israel should be. Among the passive disciples who did not protest, there was one who must have felt, more than Peter even, very ill at ease. The evangelist expressly notes that all this took place when the devil had already prompted Judas Iscariot to betray Jesus. When the footwashing was completed, Jesus openly highlighted the incomprehensible presence of the betrayer. For he knew who would betray him. So he said: 'Not all of you are clean.' Thus the humble love of the Servant spoke to all without exception, even to the one who he knew beforehand would betray him, one of the disciples to whom he had in part given his trust. Jesus could have arranged matters in such a way that Judas would have left the company of disciples before Jesus gave them this sign of love. But this was not what he wanted, for love, even when it is clearly fruitless, excludes no one; it continues to forgive, even in advance. For from no other motive than love – saving, healing love – did Jesus again and again bow before his beloved friends. No one can show greater love than he who gives his own life. No one can show greater love than he who becomes the Servant of all.

In Jesus' Church the sign of the delivered-up body and the shed blood will never be lacking, nor the sign of humble love which bows down and effaces the self. 'I have set you an example, that you also should do as I have done to you' (John 13:15).

44

Confusion and Testing

'We wish to see Jesus' – these are the words with which a few Greeks who were in sympathy with the Jewish religion pursued the disciples. With their own eyes they wanted to see this Jesus about whom they had heard so much and whom they had perhaps already pictured in their own minds. And so they saw him as he was, not in his glorified state, but in his human situation of weakness and in this time of testing (John 12:20–33).

This passage from the fourth gospel in fact offers an account of Jesus' last trial. John does not relate the story of Jesus' death-struggle in the Garden of Gethsemane. He tells of another temptation and accompanying death-struggle. Nevertheless this story began with Jesus' solemn announcement that his hour had come: 'The hour has come for the Son of Man to be glorified' (12:23). And this glorification – Jesus does not doubt it for a second – necessarily comes through death: 'Very truly, I tell you, unless a grain of wheat falls into the earth and dies, it remains just a single grain; but if it dies, it bears much fruit' (12:24).

Suddenly the discourse stops. After a brief silence, which seems like an eternity, Jesus resumes his speech in a tone which betrays intense emotion, almost a sort of panic. 'Now my soul is troubled. And what should I say – "Father, save me from this hour"?' Jesus is deeply moved, disturbed, almost desperate. How is this possible? What is going on inside him? 'I am deeply grieved, even to death,' he says in the gospel of Matthew (26:38). The reference in John's gospel is to the same dread and the same temptation. And as he did in the three accounts of the temptation of Gethsemane, Jesus here begs his Father that this hour and this cup might pass from him: 'Father save me from this hour.' But just as he did in Gethsemane, Jesus here immediately takes his words back and surrenders to the tender will of the Father: 'But it is precisely for this reason that I have come to this hour. Father, glorify your name' (John 12:27–8). In other words, your will be done, not mine.

We wish to see Jesus! Indeed. But the only Jesus we can see here is the Jesus who is on his way to his passion and death, the Jesus who is 'gasping for air', deeply afraid, as we would be in his place; it is the Jesus who is deeply disturbed and tempted, who despite his 'loud cries and tears' (Heb. 5:7) was not spared a single human trial or test, not even death.

But Jesus came to us precisely for this hour, this desperation and this death, in order once and for all to save us from temptation and death. And how? By inviting us to follow in his footsteps, to travel with him the same inescapable road to the same suffering and the same Easter.

After speaking of the grain of wheat which had to die in order not to remain a single grain, Jesus added: 'Whoever would serve me must follow me and where I am, there will my servant be also.' No servant of Jesus will be spared desperation or testing. Therefore all who are his disciples must allow themselves to be seized by Jesus; therefore, they must decide to place their feet in Jesus' footprints.

In the matter of this fundamental choice, the choice every Christian makes, there is little difference among the true servants of Jesus. The way of the servant in the monastery is hardly more difficult than that of the servant in the world.

And the way of the servant in the world is not easier than the way of the servant in the monastery. Their respective ways are simply different; the foundation and the end result are the same – the Easter of Jesus. Not a single servant of Jesus will ever be relieved of having to follow the Master to that point, to the narrow entrance, the tumultuous narrows of Easter, the narrows of temptation and death, where everyone in turn will enter when their hour has come.

But there is no doubt that Jesus will save us and see us through the narrows. It is precisely for that hour of desperation *and* enormous confidence, after all, that we live: 'Father, glorify your name.'

45

Passing Away in Love

All three of them were there: John, the disciple whom Jesus loved, plus the holy women, his mother Mary and Mary Magdalene. Together they had spent the evening and the night, completely shaken by Jesus' arrest in the garden, by the insistent insinuations of the maidservants which caused Peter to fall, and by the bullying of the military personnel along the path of the condemned. Thus they had arrived at Golgotha where they stood beneath the cross of Jesus. As they endured all these things, it was no longer to *receive* Jesus' love, but to show their love to him in turn and, with the greatest possible human tenderness, to stand by him in his death-struggle.

There is first of all his mother, Mary, the woman who nurtured him with loving care when he was still very small, whose delight it was to cherish him and to envelop him with the dearest maternal tenderness. In a little while she would again take him on her lap and press him to her heart, in order for the last time to embrace this body, flesh of her flesh, but this time, as he rested in death, it would be with tears and laments.

Then there is Mary Magdalene, the penitent sinner who loved Jesus so intensely that one fine day, at a single stroke, all her sins were forgiven. Our liturgy confuses her – fortunately, we might be inclined to say – with that other Mary, Mary of Bethany, who, John tells us, was much loved by Jesus. These two women, accordingly, had the privilege of washing Jesus' feet, as his mother had so often done many years before. Both women had also ventured to dry his feet with their beautiful long hair and to anoint them with costly ointment. To the care of their loving heart and hands Jesus entrusted his forthcoming burial. For it was with an eye to his burial, he explained, that they performed this costly anointing.

And then there is John, the mysterious disciple whom Jesus loved in particular and who often sat next to him at table. It was he who took the liberty of leaning against Jesus' chest, as the author of the fourth gospel says, using the same expression he employed in the prologue where he describes the Word as being 'in the bosom of the Father'. This is a most moving picture of Jesus' love, a love he simultaneously receives from his heavenly Father and bestows upon his friends here on earth.

Only this trio, with much love, followed him into his final hour. With hearts full of tenderness they were with Jesus when he was about to die, to pass from the one love to the other, from the perishable signs here to the unfolding reality of the hereafter, but always in the same unique love. Before yielding to it, however, Jesus still had to perform one last act of love, the only one of which he was still capable from his position on the cross. 'When Jesus saw his mother and the disciple whom he loved standing beside her, he said to his mother, "Woman, here is your son". Then he said to his disciple, "Here is your mother" ' (John 19:26–7).

From that moment on, as far as Jesus was concerned, death, the fulfilment of everything, was free to make its entry. Love had exhausted him and he had exhausted it. The moment had come for him to take his leave of this human tenderness, a tenderness which had accompanied him to the very end: the infinite tenderness of a mother, the intense passion of the sinner who had been healed by Jesus' love, the tender affection of the elect brother. Before dying and passing into the other love of the hereafter, there was nothing left for him to do than to quietly detach himself from them and to entrust them to each other as a sign of farewell and everlasting remembrance. His mother received a new son who was an elect son of Jesus. The disciple received a new mother who was the mother of Jesus. From this point on everything was fulfilled: first of all, the Scriptures, but also the long journey of love to the end, the love Jesus had bestowed and the love he received. Now, he could bow his head and commend his spirit to his Father. His last breath was like an embrace, the first and henceforth eternal embrace in the love of the hereafter. The embrace of the Word and the Father. Since the death of Jesus, which for the first time in history was a death of love, every death resembles his: an Easter or a passage from the one love to the other, from the signs to the reality; a passage in which, like Jesus, we allow ourselves to be cradled by love and sleep in death or – which is the same – in love, in the bosom of the Father.

46

Staggering Temptation

According to the passion narrative, Jesus was twice the victim of a staggering temptation, the vertigo of sin and human weakness, which he had taken upon himself, and that of death. The first time it happened was on the Mount of Olives. The second time, which was even worse, was when he hung on the cross. Just as when he endured the temptations in the wilderness, Jesus repeatedly faced a dizzying temptation by himself, totally left to his fate, mysteriously alone.

Yet, on the Mount of Olives, he had invited Peter, James and John, his three most faithful disciples, to stay with him and to follow him into the very heart of the testing. Alas, it was a wasted effort, for they were not going to go with him that far. Their waking and praying were but of short duration. Sleep soon overpowered them, although the moment seemed well chosen, for never before had their unanimity around Jesus seemed so impressive. When Jesus had earlier announced to them that he, the shepherd, would be smitten and that they, the sheep, would be miserably scattered, they had seemed so marvellously united around their Master. They had all endorsed Peter's ringing statement: 'Even though I must die with you, I will not deny you!' (Matt. 26:35).

Yet Jesus is now totally alone with his Father, grieved and agitated, as he acknowledged to his disciples, though he needed their presence as never before. He even begged them: 'Remain here and stay awake with me.' Overcome by confusion and shattered by the prospect of his approaching death, he again found himself alone before the Father. After his plea to his disciples he now prayed to his Father. 'My Father, if it is possible, let this cup pass from me.' But then he added, 'yet not what I want but what you want'. What else can he say? He and his Father after all were one. But still it remains a painful mystery. For Jesus' confusion persists and everything that goes on in him during his prayer of surrender continually rebels against the prospect of the death that is stealing upon him.

His confusion in fact continued. A few hours later it was more dizzying still when Jesus, hanging from the cross, uttered the painful cry from the psalm: 'Eli, Eli, [my God, my God] lama [why] sabachthani [are you forsaking me]?' Beyond and through Jesus' confusion – a confusion caused by the total abandonment in which his Father left him in this hour – Jesus' will more than ever before coincided with that of the Father. Only a few witnesses took note of that other verse from the psalm: 'Father, into your hands I commend my spirit.' Most of them heard only the heart-rending cry when he died. A cry of horror or a cry of love – who can tell? Or was it perhaps the cry for a new birth, the cry by which the exhausted body of Jesus raised itself one more time in order forever to embrace his Father as he gave up his spirit?

Since that long-gone time when Jesus once and for all endured the vertigo of all our temptations, we are no longer simply called to witness; we are now also acting persons. No temptation or pain which was first endured, quieted or healed by Jesus can still strike us. Only our confusion remains, but now it is filled by the power and extreme tenderness of Jesus.

47

Body and Word

To be able to recognise the risen Jesus the disciples had to go through two different but connected experiences. They had to be able to touch Jesus and their mind had to be made receptive to understanding the Scriptures (Luke 24:35–48).

The experience that Jesus really has risen and still lives today is not self-evident. The certainty of Easter is manifestly not the certainty of the things of everyday, but totally different. We see this reality also in the gospel: it seems perfectly normal to walk up to the side of the Risen Jesus without seeing him; to welcome him in one's home without recognising him; to meet him and then mistake him for the gardener.

We must first touch Jesus' body, even though it is not up to us to take the initiative to that end: 'It is I myself. Touch me and see: a spirit does not have flesh and bones' (Luke 24:39). Jesus himself presents his body to the disciples so that by touching him they would recognise him. He also takes the initiative of eating a piece of grilled fish before their eyes so as to let them know that he, even as the Risen One, had remained just as human as they were.

Touching Jesus' body is a first form of recognition but it points to another experience, that is the recognition via the Scriptures. At this point the disciples were poorer by far than when it was only a matter of seeing or touching Jesus' body. Certainly they could read the Scriptures. They read and knew them and, in addition, interpreted them to the best of their ability. But, like all the Jews, they were totally unable up to that point to discover Jesus in them. Left to themselves, they only understood the Bible according to the letter and, apart from Jesus' Easter, it simply remained a dead letter.

Then Jesus again took the initiative: 'These are my words that I spoke to you while I was still with you – that everything written about me in the law of Moses, the prophets, and the psalms must be fulfilled. Then he opened their minds to understand the Scriptures' (Luke 24:44–5). Thus, the disciples received their first catechetical instruction after Easter, their first lesson in authentic Christian theology even, and it was straight from Jesus' own mouth. He alone, after all, could open their minds and hearts to the integral meaning of the Bible, to the meaning put into it from the start but which for a long time remained hidden, only to be unveiled at Jesus' 'crossing over', by the living touch of the incarnate Word, and by the living body of the written Word.

The same adventure occurred in the lives of the two disciples on the way to Emmaus to whom the stranger, whom they met on the road, explained the Scriptures at length. They had the same intimate experience when in a particularly spirited way the Word was opened up to them: 'Were not our hearts burning within us while he was talking to us on the road, while he was opening the Scriptures to us?'

It is still that way now; those who are called to recognise the Risen Jesus do so by following the same two-pronged path: by the sacrament of Jesus' body and that of his Word, touching Jesus' body and understanding the Scriptures. These two sacraments, in a mysterious way, contain the

Risen One and at the same time in every Eucharist make him present to all who believe.

How could we ever believe if Jesus himself did not take the initiative to make it happen? How would we recognise Jesus in the sacrament of his body and blood if he himself did not invite us to do this and if he did not tenderly wound our heart at the moment we received him? How would we find the Risen One in his Word if he himself did not open our mind and set our heart on fire every time he spoke to us through the Scriptures? In our own heart, which leaps up with joy, we recognise Jesus, the Jesus who is risen and still lives, even in our midst.

48

Believing without Seeing

All these things were recorded in his book, writes St John, 'so that you may come to believe that Jesus is the Messiah, the Son of God' (John 20:19–31; spec. v. 31). Hence the sign announced to us in the gospel is a sign of unbelief, unbelief like the apostle Thomas' lack of faith.

Nor does this concern only Thomas, for the other disciples were no quicker than he was to figure things out. Despite the witness of those to whom Jesus had already appeared, they were still ensconcing themselves behind locked doors, paralysed by fear of the Jews. It was only when Jesus himself appeared to them and showed them his hands and his side that they recognised him.

More remarkable still, of course, is what happened in the case of Thomas. For him the three years he had travelled around with Jesus were not enough to allow him to take his fellow disciples at their word. Not only did he, like the others, want to see Jesus with his own eyes, but he wanted to touch Jesus' body as well. He demanded irrefutable proof that Jesus was no longer dead but alive. Thomas wanted first to see and touch, something very different from the faith upon which Jesus pronounced his beatitude. The faith of Thomas and the other apostles will presumably always differ from ours. After their initial doubts, they became eyewitnesses of Jesus' resurrection. The story of their doubts and problems in recognising Jesus and their sudden certainty afterwards all constitutes the foundation of our faith. All these things were recorded in the book, writes St John, so that we also might come to believe.

The faith of the apostles, including that of Thomas, was not really all that remarkable: they had seen. The real miracle, the one that would continually happen over and over, is the faith of all those others who came after Jesus' immediate disciples and never saw anything. That is the faith Jesus emphatically commends when he responds to Thomas' exclamation of faith: 'Have you believed because you have seen me? *Blessed are those who have not seen and yet have come to believe.*'

Blessed are those who believe without having seen! In them, after all, the power of Easter bears fruit day after day. Those who have not seen the empty tomb, who never met Jesus in the garden, who never heard the sound of his voice, who could never put their hands in his wounds, see very differently since it has been given them to believe before seeing: they will see in the measure in which they have believed.

But how? If one were to ask them, they would undoubtedly not be able to answer. For what do they know about the Risen Lord? Everything and nothing. They cannot describe the colour of his hair or the tint of his skin. They have not, after all, seen him in the way Thomas and the others saw him. Still they know him almost better than if one day they had met him on a street corner. They love him infinitely more than if they had only walked by his side on the roads of Galilee. Without having seen him they believe in him and love him without seeing him. And that, precisely, is faith. Often it fell unexpectedly into their lap and always without a 'how' or a 'why'. They thought they had for years possessed the faith when suddenly it blossomed, it sprang up, it lit up and became alive as Jesus lives today. Often it arises solely from a word in the gospel, simply as we listen to a story, sometimes in response to a sign from the Risen Lord which touches and wounds our heart.

That is our faith, especially the faith of the humblest person among believers; that is the first Easter miracle and perhaps the greatest, the real proof that Jesus has risen. This faith will move mountains; this faith, which has overcome the world, will receive whatever it asks for: 'Blessed are those who have not seen and yet have come to believe' (John 20:29).

49

A Length Ahead

'He is risen from the dead' is the message which Mary Magdalene and the other Mary received to pass on to the disciples and to us all (John 20:1–18, Matt. 27:56). Death has been conquered: the death of Jesus has once and for all become the victory over death. So Jesus lives! He has triumphed over death, but how? Simply because it was a death motivated by love. 'On account of his love as the Son', comments the author of the Letter to the Hebrews, Jesus' cries and tears were heard and seen in the time of his suffering. At sight of his Son being crucified for love's sake the heart of his Father broke. 'He could not give him over to Sheol; he could not inflict this injury on him' (see Ps. 16:10). 'The Lord has punished me severely, but he did not give me over to death' (Ps. 118:18). Love crossed the boundary of death and raised the living one from the grave.

Inasmuch as this was love's masterpiece, Easter can only become visible to eyes that are filled with love. Hence the message of the Risen One was first of all entrusted to those who were closest to Jesus, who had loved him and been loved by him, as though he were too vulnerable in the hands of others. The first witnesses of the resurrection are not the apostles, even though they would later become the witnesses of his resurrection *par excellence*. But they were not these witnesses from the first moment. Would they have recognised Jesus? Or would they have imagined they were seeing a ghost, like that time they were caught in a storm on the lake (Mark 6:45–52)?

In any case the first fruits of the resurrection were reserved for those who looked with the eyes of their heart and saw what the others could not yet see.

The first, accordingly, were the women, among whom was Mary Magdalene. They had no doubts whatsoever. An apostle, confronted with an empty tomb, would certainly first have examined the place and the circumstances and insisted on proof. The women, on the other hand, immediately gave credit to the words of the angel. Trembling with emotion and filled with joy they hurried to pass on the message to the apostles, but these men gave the women, with their 'idle tale', a cool reception, as Luke notes (24:11). On top of this there was yet another surprise, though it was hardly a surprise. When an unfamiliar figure in the garden suddenly pronounced her name, Mary immediately recognised Jesus. How? Exclusively by picking up the accent of love, by that deep outrushing longing. Could one possibly imagine a more intimate relationship between two persons who loved each other than by hearing a first name pronounced with such unmistakable uniqueness? She who loved him could certainly not expect a more glorious proof of his resurrection. Her first name, spoken with love and tenderness, meant more than a million instances of proof.

Among the apostles there was one exception: a man who understood when everyone else was still in doubt, who had insight when the others were still without a clue – John, the disciple whom Jesus loved. In the matter of recognising Jesus, love is always one length ahead of the rest. When Peter entered the empty tomb before John, what he saw astonished and confused him, but that's as far as it went. When John went in after him, he 'saw and believed, for as yet they did not understand the scripture', says the gospel (John 20:8–9). John was similarly the first to recognize the stranger who was grilling fish on the beach after a heavy night's catch of fish. Intuitively he guessed: 'It is the Lord.'

Love was the first to recognize Jesus. To the others, and to us all, it predicted that we too would see him: 'Go and tell the brothers they must go to Galilee – back to their homes and work – and there they will see me.' We can trust the love of Mary Magdalene for only love is trustworthy, their love and ours as well, though barely awakened and always threatened; still it exists, it is there, however humble and small. And to the mind of love a little means a lot. The dear name of the Risen Jesus which lives in our heart and on our tongue, and our Christian name which he softly whispers in the ear of our heart, mean more than all the proof in the world.

50

Our Deepest Dimension

In the gospel Jesus speaks of two dimensions which together make up every one of us: our exteriority and our interiority, the outside and the inside of our being (Mark 7:1–23). And Jesus came to the conclusion that some believing people in his day showed interest only in the exterior and little or none in the interior dimension. They spent an enormous amount of energy on the adornment of the external and very little on that which lies behind it. They were content to tidy up the façade of their life and did not worry about the interior, their own heart.

This attitude is all the more regrettable, says Jesus, because there is frequently a gaping disparity between the outer and the inner part of a person. The external sometimes seems seductive but the reality hidden behind it is often wretched and even repulsive. Jesus mentions 'whited sepulchres', beautiful to look at on the outside, but full of corruption within. Every human is at liberty to be content with this disparity and simply to ignore it. Appearances are fine and very promising and that's where we usually leave things. We very easily take pleasure in them also because other people often consider us fortunate on account of them. Some people may possess charisma, even gain a following, but their 'magic' somehow does not come straight from the heart. Their inner decay manifests itself only much later, often quite unexpectedly, and sometimes to everyone's astonishment.

Such disparity exists between the outer and the inner dimension in every person; it is something like a hereditary weak spot, one of the most telling consequences of the first sin. People hide themselves, no longer behind fig leaves, but behind an attitude which is externally impeccable. No one escapes this hereditary weakness. Jesus already knew that this is not a lack of nobility or intelligence; it is a weakness inherent in every human being, one that always includes the possibility of drifting away because one's heart has never been touched.

So what is Jesus' advice? It is clear from what he says that the interior, the heart of a person, is infinitely more important than the exterior, the public posture and actions. Jesus does not conclude, however, that one ought to neglect the outward things. Speaking to the Pharisees in the same context for that matter, he says: 'it is these you ought to have practised without neglecting the others' (Luke 11:42), hence both must be tended at once. One must take care of external things, but above all things of the heart. Why is that? Even though the healing of the heart does not automatically follow from our concern for the externals, the latter is extremely necessary inasmuch as it will gradually be transformed by the healed heart. It must shine and must expel all mere appearance. But how does this work? How does the transition from the outward to the inward come about? How does one find the way? From what source does this passage proceed?

This, precisely, is the mystery of our conversion day after day, the work of God in us, the greatest of all miracles. No human techniques can help us here, for human devices can only block the road. Only God can give a new direction to our inwardness. He will lead us to the discovery of the treasure that lies hidden in our heart, aside from all the rules, even without the rules, but nevertheless somewhere in the heart of every life rule. This treasure is the life of the Spirit within us, which enables us to live each moment and in the end takes us where we never wished to go, where all external rules cease to exist, where even the finest exterior becomes unimportant by comparison with the light that shines from within.

From now on, though these external rules and laws will not be abolished, they will no longer oppress us; they will have been fulfilled, brought to their completion, as Jesus tells us (Matt. 5:17). They will only be instruments and we can without risk put them aside if God wants to use them in and through us to radiate his love to the outside world, to teach all people how easy his yoke is and how light his burden, for a heart that opens itself to love.